SUZANNE BYRD

Tame Your Brain, Tidy Your Life

An ADHD Woman's Blueprint for (Mostly) Organized Days

First published by Mental Health Publishing 2025

Copyright © 2025 by Suzanne Byrd

All rights reserved. No part of this publication may be reproduced, stored or transmitted in any form or by any means, electronic, mechanical, photocopying, recording, scanning, or otherwise without written permission from the publisher. It is illegal to copy this book, post it to a website, or distribute it by any other means without permission.

First edition

This book was professionally typeset on Reedsy.
Find out more at reedsy.com

Contents

1	So... What's the Big Deal with ADHD Anyway?	1
2	Embrace the Quirks, Toss the Shame	5
3	Turning Brain Fog into Brain Focus	15
4	The Power of (Tiny) Habits	27
5	Mindset Magic—From Negative Loops to Positive Pep-Talks	39
6	Dealing with Decision Paralysis	50
7	Procrastination Rehab 101	63
8	Who Moved My Keys? Mindful Organization for Women With...	76
9	Finding Your Flow in Work & Personal Projects	88
10	Celebrate the (Imperfect) Wins	100

1

So... What's the Big Deal with ADHD Anyway?

There's a moment many women experience—often in their late twenties, thirties, or even well into midlife—when they realize, "Hey, my brain doesn't quite work like everyone else's." Maybe you've known you have ADHD for a while, maybe it's a brand-new discovery, or maybe you're still on the fence. Whichever the case, you're here, curious about how to corral the chaos and create some semblance of tidy calm in your life. Welcome to the club!

ADHD 101 (A Quick Refresher)

Attention Deficit Hyperactivity Disorder is, at its core, a neurodevelopmental condition that affects your ability to regulate attention, manage impulses, and organize tasks. Contrary to popular stereotypes, it's not just about getting distracted by shiny things (though, let's be honest, that happens too). For many women, ADHD can manifest as:

- **Chronic Disorganization**: Feeling like your life is in a perpetual state of "Where did I put my keys/phone/wallet/dignity?"
- **Emotional Overload**: Cycling between feeling supercharged to tackle the world and feeling like everything is too overwhelming—even the laundry.
- **Hyperfocus**: Zoning in on something so intently (a new craft, Netflix series, or that must-read book about the mating rituals of seahorses) that you forget the world outside your tunnel of fascination.

Why ADHD Looks Different for Women

Women often slip through the diagnostic cracks because we're socialized to mask our symptoms, stay "polite," and somehow keep the ship afloat. There's also the reality that many healthcare professionals historically looked for the more classic (read: male) presentation of ADHD, characterized by overt hyperactivity. As a result, countless women were told they were just "scatterbrained," "lazy," or "emotional."

- **Masking**: You might've become a professional at seeming calm and collected on the outside, while internally you're thinking: *Did I respond to that email? Wait, was I supposed to send a birthday card? Oh, the cat just threw up. How do I fix my entire life by 2 p.m.?*
- **Misdiagnosis**: Before learning about ADHD, many women are diagnosed with anxiety, depression, or mood disorders—which can be co-occurring but aren't always the whole story.
- **Multitasking Myths**: We're told women are "great at mul-

titasking," so if you can't juggle 37 tasks simultaneously, it feels like a personal failing, not a sign that your brain wiring differs from the so-called norm.

The Organization Struggle Is Real

You know that feeling of walking into a room to do something, only to forget why you're there? That's a classic ADHD moment. Now multiply that by a hundred: The hamper is overflowing, there's a half-eaten sandwich on the counter, your best friend texted you an hour ago about tonight's dinner reservations, and you're late for a meeting. If that sounds familiar, you're in the right place.

But here's the good news: ADHD isn't just about challenges. Many women with ADHD are creative problem-solvers, empathetic friends, and masters of thinking outside the box. The trick is learning to harness the positive aspects of ADHD while putting guardrails around the negative ones.

What "Mostly Organized" Looks Like

Let's address the elephant in the room: The title promises "(Mostly) Organized Days." Notice how it doesn't say "perfectly" or "Pinterest-level." That's on purpose. Achieving a color-coded, alphabetized pantry might be a lovely goal, but aiming for "good enough" organization—where you can find what you need most of the time without spiraling into meltdown mode—is a more realistic (and much kinder) target.

- **Progress Over Perfection**: If you can locate the car keys, remember to pay your bills, and cut down on panic-induced

rummaging through the junk drawer, you're already winning.
- **Consistent Tweaks**: ADHD management is a lifetime practice, not a one-and-done checklist. You'll tweak and refine your systems as you go.

Sneak Peek at What's Coming

In the chapters ahead, we'll talk about building small, sustainable habits, tackling that sense of constant overwhelm, and finding your personal style of organization. Expect step-by-step strategies, mindset shifts, and the occasional self-deprecating joke (because if we don't laugh about trying to find the phone that's literally in our hand, we might cry).

- **Chapter 2: Embrace the Quirks, Toss the Shame**: We'll dive deeper into reframing ADHD-related self-criticism.
- **Chapter 3: Turning Brain Fog into Brain Focus**: Tips for managing distractibility and staying on task (ish).
- …and so on, right down to tackling real-world tasks like laundry mountains and the dreaded "junk mail vortex."

Quick Action Step

Before we move on, take a moment to congratulate yourself on picking up this book. Seriously. You've made a choice to invest in understanding your brain better, and that's huge. If you're in an environment where you can, put your hand on your heart (or do a little victory dance) and say, "I'm allowed to learn new ways to handle my ADHD, and I'm doing a great job so far."

Because you really are.

2

Embrace the Quirks, Toss the Shame

Picture this: You're standing in the middle of your living room, where piles of laundry, half-finished craft projects, and an embarrassingly large collection of mismatched socks surround you. Instead of feeling motivated to tackle the mess, you sense a pit forming in your stomach. You think, *"Why can't I get it together? Everyone else seems to manage just fine. What's wrong with me?"* That, my friend, is the voice of shame—one of the biggest obstacles you'll face while trying to organize your ADHD life.

The trouble with ADHD isn't always about losing keys or forgetting appointments. Often, the deepest struggle happens in your own head, where a relentless internal commentator insists you're failing at something everyone else apparently mastered decades ago. In this chapter, we'll explore the roots of that shame, why it's especially potent for women with ADHD, and how to replace self-criticism with a gentler, more constructive approach.

The Shame Spiral: A Vicious (and Familiar) Cycle

For many women, shame sneaks in under the guise of "Shouldn't you be better at this by now?" or "You're just not trying hard enough." It's a harsh narrative that can turn everyday slip-ups—like forgetting to move the clothes from the washer to the dryer—into evidence of personal failure. The cycle goes something like this:

1. **A "Fail" Moment:** You forget an important date, run late to work, or misplace your child's field trip form *again*.
2. **Self-Blame and Guilt:** "I'm so irresponsible. I can't believe I messed this up."
3. **Shame Attack:** "Everyone else can do this—what's wrong with me? If people find out, they'll think I'm incompetent."
4. **Avoidance or Overcompensation:** You might try to bury your head in the sand to forget the embarrassment, or swing the other way and become hypervigilant to prove you're not a failure.

This shame spiral is more than just feeling bad; it can become a self-fulfilling prophecy. When you're weighed down by constant shame, it's hard to find the energy or optimism to tackle new challenges. Ironically, you may end up avoiding the very systems and strategies that could help you manage your ADHD more effectively.

The Female Factor: Why Women Feel It So Intensely

Society has a funny way of handing out scripts to women: *You should be organized, nurturing, and on top of your game—whether that's at work, at home, or both.* The cultural expectation often implies that any deviation from near-perfection is a moral failing, not just a quirk of neurology.

- **Cultural Conditioning:** Growing up, many of us learned that "good girls" keep tidy rooms, meet deadlines, remember birthdays, and generally ensure life runs smoothly for themselves and others. If your ADHD brain doesn't cooperate, you might feel like you're violating some unwritten social contract.
- **Pressure to Appear Competent:** Because of underdiagnosis or late diagnosis, a lot of women operate under the assumption that everyone else is simply more capable. When your brain can't keep up with all those demands, shame can burn even more intensely.
- **Comparisons with "Perfect" Peers:** Thanks to social media, we're constantly bombarded with photos of immaculate desks, color-coded planners, and smiling mothers who never seem frazzled. It's easy to forget those curated images don't reflect real life.

For women, the shame narrative isn't just about personal struggle; it ties into larger societal standards. Recognizing that fact—*and questioning it*—is an important step in dismantling shame from the ground up.

It's Not a Character Flaw, It's Brain Wiring

One critical realization about ADHD is that it's rooted in how your brain is wired, not a moral failure or laziness. The ADHD brain often has *executive functioning* challenges, meaning tasks like organizing, planning, and prioritizing can feel like climbing Mount Everest without oxygen. Meanwhile, you might excel at creative problem-solving or empathizing with others, strengths that non-ADHD folks might struggle to cultivate.

In other words, ADHD is a **neurological variation**, not a personal failing. When you reframe your struggles through that lens, you can begin trading shame for curiosity: *Why do I struggle with this, and what can I do about it?* Curiosity encourages you to experiment with new strategies instead of drowning in self-recrimination.

The Power of Self-Compassion

Countering shame involves treating yourself with the same kindness you'd extend to a dear friend. This concept, often referred to as *self-compassion*, might feel awkward or self-indulgent at first, especially if you're used to being hard on yourself. But consider how you'd react if your best friend called you in tears, saying she messed up her schedule yet again and feels like a hopeless failure. You'd likely respond with empathy, reassurance, and constructive suggestions—not a lecture on how incompetent she is. So why not practice that on yourself?

Three Components of Self-Compassion (According to Dr. Kristin Neff)

1. **Mindfulness**: Acknowledge your feelings of frustration or disappointment without exaggerating them. "I'm feeling upset because I forgot a deadline, and that's understandable."
2. **Common Humanity**: Remind yourself that everyone struggles. "I'm not the only person who's ever missed a deadline. Mistakes happen; it's part of being human."
3. **Self-Kindness**: Offer yourself comfort and understanding. "It's okay. This doesn't define me. I can learn from this and move forward."

When you swap shame-laden self-talk for gentle encouragement, you free up mental and emotional energy to actually solve the problem at hand.

Banishing the Perfectionism Parasite

Perfectionism is often the bedfellow of shame, especially for women with ADHD. The thought process goes something like, *If I can just do everything perfectly, no one will see my flaws, and I won't have to feel incompetent.* The problem is, perfectionism sets an impossible standard, and when you inevitably fall short, the shame rears its head again, mocking you for not meeting those sky-high expectations.

- **Recognize the All-or-Nothing Trap**: Often, perfectionists see tasks in black-and-white terms—either you do it flawlessly, or you fail miserably. But the reality is, life is full of

gray areas, and doing something at 80% is still doing it.
- **Practice "Good Enough"**: Aim for *incremental improvements*. If you can reduce the chaos by 30%, that's still a win. This is especially crucial for ADHD brains, which can become overwhelmed by large, undefined goals.
- **Reward Partial Progress**: Instead of fixating on what's incomplete, celebrate small victories—like filing half your paperwork or organizing one shelf. Momentum builds on itself when you acknowledge each step forward.

Reducing perfectionist tendencies can help you detach your self-worth from your organizational successes (or slip-ups). Remember, your value doesn't hinge on how neatly your spice rack is labeled.

Turning Down the Volume on Negative Self-Talk

If your inner monologue is stuck on a loop of "I'm such a mess," "I'll never get this right," or "I'm just lazy," it's time to change the channel. Negative self-talk rarely motivates long-term growth; instead, it paralyzes you with shame and self-doubt.

Strategies to Rewire Your Inner Monologue

1. **Name That Voice**: Give your inner critic a silly name or persona. The next time it starts spewing negativity, you can say, "Okay, *Negative Nancy*, I hear you, but I'm choosing to focus on solutions right now."
2. **Flip the Script**: Whenever you catch a self-deprecating thought, counter it with a more balanced perspective. "I'm not lazy—I just struggle with executive functioning, and

I'm learning strategies to help me."
3. **Use Journals or Sticky Notes**: Write down affirmations or realistic counter-statements to your negative thoughts. Stick them on your bathroom mirror or computer monitor so you see them often.

You might feel cheesy or inauthentic at first, but over time, these small efforts can shift your baseline attitude toward a more supportive mindset.

Leaning into Your ADHD Superpowers

Yes, ADHD can make life tricky. But it also has some perks, often overlooked amid the chaos. By recognizing and amplifying your strengths, you can build a foundation of self-confidence that helps buffer against shame when things go awry.

- **Creativity & Imagination**: ADHD brains can leap to ideas and connections that others might miss. Use this to your advantage when tackling organizational challenges—brainstorm unconventional storage solutions, for instance.
- **Hyperfocus**: While it can be a double-edged sword, hyperfocus can be harnessed for productivity. Once you've identified a task that genuinely intrigues you, you can accomplish a lot in a short time.
- **Empathy & Sensitivity**: Many women with ADHD report heightened sensitivity to others' emotions. This can make you an excellent friend, partner, or coworker who truly connects with people's feelings.

Leaning into your superpowers helps you build a sense of

worth and competence that can coexist with any organizational struggles you're working through.

Creating an Uplifting Environment

Sometimes, shame can be fueled by the people or settings around us. If you're surrounded by individuals who ridicule your forgetfulness or belittle your efforts, it's much harder to move forward. Conversely, if your environment is filled with supportive voices and resources, you're more likely to flourish.

Take a Relationship Inventory

- **Supporters**: Who encourages and respects you, flaws and all? Keep these folks close.
- **Energy Drainers**: Who constantly points out your shortcomings or dismisses ADHD as an "excuse"? If possible, set boundaries or reduce their influence.
- **Online & Offline Communities**: Look for ADHD support groups (in-person or virtual) where you can exchange tips, stories, and camaraderie. Hearing others say, "Me too!" can be incredibly healing.

Physical Space Matters Too

- **Visual Reminders**: Use whiteboards, corkboards, or sticky notes to keep track of tasks so they don't evaporate from your memory. Display empowering quotes or affirmations to balance out negative self-talk.
- **Create "Safe Zones"**: Designate a corner of your house for decompressing—a comfy chair with minimal distractions,

calming scents, and maybe a pair of noise-canceling headphones.
- **Celebrate Your Style**: If bright colors and whimsical décor spark joy and help you stay engaged, go for it! Make your space reflect who you are, not who you think you *should* be.

Action Steps: Putting Shame in Its Place

1. **Shame Journal**: For one week, jot down moments when you feel shame creep in. What triggered it? What was your reaction? Simply noticing patterns can strip shame of some of its power.
2. **Affirmation Exercise**: At the end of each day, write down one thing you did well (even if it's just getting out of bed on time or replying to an important email). Focus on progress, not perfection.
3. **Share With a Safe Person**: Whether it's a therapist, a friend who "gets it," or an online ADHD forum, talking about shame can be liberating. Often, you'll discover others share the same struggles.

The Road Ahead: A Kinder Journey

Embracing your ADHD quirks doesn't mean resigning yourself to a life of endless clutter or chaos. It means acknowledging that you have unique hurdles and equally unique strengths. By loosening the grip of shame, you open up space in your life for real solutions—like habit-building, time-management hacks, and organization systems that actually make sense for your brain.

This chapter is all about setting a new emotional baseline.

Instead of feeling perpetually "less than," you can operate from a place of compassionate curiosity. Next time you find yourself buried in a pile of misplaced items or overdue tasks, ask, *"How can I adjust my environment or approach so this doesn't keep happening?"* Rather than, *"Ugh, why am I such a mess?"* The difference might seem subtle, but it's seismic in how it shapes your emotions, motivation, and willingness to try again.

In **Chapter 3**, we'll explore how to transform that lingering brain fog into clearer, more focused thinking. We'll look at practical strategies for staying on task—at least long enough to accomplish what matters most. Until then, pat yourself on the back (seriously, do it) for showing up, reading this, and being open to seeing your ADHD through a kinder, more empowering lens.

You're not broken—you're just wired differently. And in that difference lies all the creativity, curiosity, and compassion that make you *you*. When shame knocks on the door, remind it that you've got better things to do, like forging a life where your quirks are something to celebrate, not conceal.

3

Turning Brain Fog into Brain Focus

On a random Tuesday afternoon, you find yourself staring at your computer screen. One tab open for work email, another for your personal messages, a third for that must-buy gift for your niece's birthday, and a fourth featuring a deep dive into cake-decorating videos (because apparently, that's what your brain decided to fixate on). You know you've got a list of tasks waiting, but your mind feels like a screen with 27 tabs open and the music from one of those tabs playing on a mysterious loop in the background. Welcome to the ADHD brain fog—where mental clutter, distractions, and hyperactive ideas collide in a swirling storm of "Wait, what was I doing again?"

In this chapter, we'll explore why ADHD brains are so prone to this phenomenon and, more importantly, how you can tame the chaos. Think of it as giving your brain a well-deserved tune-up: we'll walk through strategies to reduce mental noise, stay anchored in the moment, and find your way back to focus when you inevitably drift into tangential daydreams about crocheting a sweater for your dog.

Why ADHD Brains Fog Out

ADHD isn't just about being easily distracted by the outside world. It's also about the *internal* collisions of ideas, memories, anxieties, and random tangents that pop into your mind without warning. If you've ever caught yourself mid-email and suddenly remembered you need to check if you paid the electric bill, then pivoted to search for a new lamp, only to get sucked into an online sale on throw pillows—congratulations, you've experienced the ADHD thought spiral.

Executive Function: A Quick Refresher

Your executive functions are mental skills that help with planning, focusing attention, juggling multiple tasks, and regulating emotions. In ADHD, some of these functions are underactive or struggle to coordinate, which can lead to:

- **Working Memory Woes**: Your short-term mental "scratchpad" loses track of important details, like what you needed from the store or how you planned to structure your presentation.
- **Filtering Difficulties**: You don't always tune out unnecessary stimuli—both external (like chatter or passing sirens) and internal (your random thoughts about last night's dream).
- **Impulse Control Hiccups**: The allure of novelty or a fun distraction can yank you from your current task before you even realize what's happening.

Emotional Distress and Fog

It's not just about the immediate environment or your to-do list. If you're carrying emotional baggage—stress at work, relationship worries, or shame from repeated "failures"—those anxieties can clog your mental gears, amplifying the fog. This emotional static can heighten distractibility, making it even tougher to find that elusive zone of focus.

Step 1: Tame Mental Clutter

We often think of clutter as physical objects strewn around the house. However, mental clutter—unfinished tasks swirling in your head, anxious to-dos, random thoughts—can be just as overwhelming.

The Brain Dump Technique

One of the simplest ways to manage mental clutter is through a **brain dump**—literally writing down everything that's been rattling inside your noggin. No sorting, no overthinking, just put pen to paper (or fingers to keyboard) and let it flow.

1. **Set Aside 5–10 Minutes**: Find a quiet spot, or at least a reasonably uninterrupted corner of your world.
2. **Write It All**: Groceries you need, texts you owe friends, project ideas, vacation plans, worries—everything.
3. **Scan for Gems**: After the stream-of-consciousness scribble, circle or highlight key tasks or important thoughts.
4. **Prioritize**: Transfer those essentials into a proper list or digital planner, ranking them by urgency or importance.

The magic of a brain dump is that it frees up your working memory. Instead of mentally juggling 15 reminders, you now have them safely captured somewhere tangible.

Establish a Daily Download Time

Instead of waiting until you're frantic, try scheduling a daily or weekly "download." Some people prefer doing it first thing in the morning; others like a bedtime release so they can sleep with a clearer mind. By integrating this into your routine, you'll steadily reduce the barrage of mental to-dos that hijack your focus.

Step 2: Optimize Your Environment

Your surroundings can either support or sabotage your efforts to concentrate. If every corner of your workspace screams "Look at me!" your already-distracted ADHD brain will struggle to stay on task.

Visual Noise Control

Let's face it: if you have 20 sticky notes plastered around your desk and a pile of paperwork from last month's project, you're essentially offering free tickets to the ADHD distraction carnival. To simplify:

- **Limit the Number of Reminders**: Keep only crucial sticky notes (like top three tasks) within eyesight, and corral the rest in a designated notebook or digital app.
- **Use Organizers or Trays**: Give items a consistent "home."

When you finish a task, put papers away immediately so they don't morph into clutter.
- **Declutter in Micro-Bursts**: Spend a quick 5-minute sprint each day clearing your desk. Over time, you'll maintain a tidier, less distracting environment.

Digital Boundaries

If physical clutter is a problem, digital clutter can be a disaster. Countless browser tabs, endless notifications, and multiple open applications can drain your focus faster than you can say, "Ooh, a new email!" Some strategies:

- **Browser Tab Discipline**: Use a browser extension that manages tabs, or limit yourself to 2–3 open at a time.
- **Notification Silencing**: Turn off nonessential alerts on your phone or computer. If you're in a deep work session, put your phone on "Do Not Disturb."
- **Task-Specific Browsers**: Create separate browser profiles—one for work, one for personal—to avoid mixing social media with work tasks.

When your environment is optimized, your brain doesn't have to constantly battle external chaos. It's like giving your attention the VIP pass to sit in a quiet, comfortable lounge instead of the noisy general admission area.

Step 3: Master the Art of Single-Tasking

ADHD is often associated with multitasking, but ironically, our brains are not built for toggling between tasks effectively. Multitasking can exacerbate brain fog by scattering your limited attention across multiple fronts.

The Pomodoro Technique (With a Twist)

The classic **Pomodoro Technique** involves working in 25-minute increments, then taking a short break. For ADHD brains, sometimes 25 minutes might be too long, or maybe you can handle longer bursts when hyperfocus kicks in. Feel free to tweak:

1. **Pick a Task**: Make it specific—"Draft the first page of my presentation slides."
2. **Set a Timer**: Choose a time frame that suits your attention span—15, 20, or even 40 minutes.
3. **Work Mindfully**: During that block, minimize distractions. Shut off notifications, close extra tabs, and focus on just that one item.
4. **Short Break**: When the timer dings, step away for a water break, quick stretch, or a few deep breaths.
5. **Rinse and Repeat**: Complete as many cycles as needed, adjusting time blocks if you find yourself losing steam.

For ADHD, it can be helpful to see the countdown visually on your screen or phone—a gentle reminder that you're in "focus mode."

The Power of "One Next Step"

Instead of tackling an entire project, zero in on the immediate next step. If you're writing a report, that next step might be "draft the introduction," not "complete the entire 20-page document." This micro-targeting keeps you from feeling overwhelmed, making it easier to slip into a focused state.

Step 4: Harness Hyperfocus Without Derailing

Hyperfocus can be both a blessing and a curse. It's that magical state where you're so absorbed that hours fly by without you noticing. While it can lead to incredible productivity (hello, finishing half a novel in a weekend!), it can also cause you to neglect crucial tasks like eating, sleeping, or picking your kid up from soccer practice.

Scheduling Hyperfocus Sessions

To make hyperfocus your ally rather than your downfall:

- **Plan Around It**: If you know you can get lost in a task, set multiple alarms to pull you out at predetermined intervals.
- **Limit Potential Collateral Damage**: Before you plunge into hyperfocus, handle any time-sensitive tasks first—like making that important phone call or feeding the dog.
- **Communicate with Others**: Let family or coworkers know you'll be "offline" for a while. That way, they won't panic when you don't respond to texts for two hours.

Watch Out for Rabbit Holes

ADHD hyperfocus isn't always job-related. Sometimes it's a deep dive into YouTube tutorials on crocheting cat sweaters. When you notice you've veered into a non-essential rabbit hole, ask: *Is this how I want to spend my hyperfocus energy?* If the answer is no, gently guide yourself back to a higher-priority task.

Step 5: Engage Your Body to Boost Your Brain

Many of us try to address focus purely by managing thoughts, but remember: ADHD can be influenced by physiological factors like sleep, nutrition, and movement. Neglecting your body's needs can worsen brain fog.

Sleep Matters. A Lot.

- **Bedtime Rituals**: Creating a pre-sleep routine—dim lights, no screens for 30 minutes, calming music—can ease your transition to rest.
- **Consistent Schedule**: Irregular sleep cycles disrupt your circadian rhythm, making focus the next day even harder.
- **Power Naps**: If you're running on fumes, a 15–20-minute nap can recharge your brain. Just keep it short to avoid grogginess.

Nutrition for the ADHD Brain

- **Protein Power**: Starting your day with protein (eggs, Greek yogurt, peanut butter) can level out your energy.
- **Steady Snacking**: Letting your blood sugar crash can intensify brain fog, so keep healthy snacks (nuts, fruit, cheese) on hand.
- **Mindful Caffeine**: A moderate amount of coffee or tea might help ADHD brains stay alert, but overdoing it can spark anxiety or jitters—both focus-killers.

Movement and Oxygen

- **Micro-Movements**: If you can't commit to a long workout, try short bursts of movement throughout the day. A brisk walk, a few jumping jacks, or a quick dance party can refresh your mind.
- **Walking Meetings**: If possible, have phone calls while walking. Physical activity can enhance focus and creativity.
- **Breathwork**: Simple breathing exercises (like 4-7-8 breathing) can lower stress hormones, clearing mental clutter.

Step 6: Forgive the Drift and Realign

Even if you follow every strategy perfectly, your ADHD brain will still wander off at times. You might glance at your phone and, 20 minutes later, realize you've been laughing at memes instead of writing that email. This is normal—especially for ADHD. The key is how you respond next.

1. **Acknowledge It**: "Oops, I drifted. No big deal."

2. **Refocus**: Identify the task at hand and pick up where you left off.
3. **Reflect**: Ask, "Why did I drift?" Maybe your environment was too noisy or your task too tedious. Adjust accordingly for next time.

This cyclical process of drifting and refocusing is part of managing ADHD. Beating yourself up only amplifies shame and stress, which worsens focus. Practice quick forgiveness and proactive solutions, and you'll find it easier to course-correct.

A Quick Mental Toolkit for Focus Emergencies

Sometimes you don't have the luxury of a calm environment or structured plan. You're on a tight deadline, or you've just had a tense argument, and your brain is swirling. Here are a few rapid-fire techniques:

- **The 5-5-5 Grounding**: Focus on 5 things you can see, 5 you can hear, and 5 you can touch or feel physically. This sensory reset can quickly anchor your mind in the present.
- **90-Second Rule**: If you're feeling overwhelmed or anxious, remind yourself that intense emotional chemistry often lasts about 90 seconds unless you fuel it with further thoughts. Take a minute and a half to breathe; let the emotion pass before deciding your next step.
- **Cold Water Splash**: Splashing cold water on your face or running your wrists under cool water can jolt you out of a foggy moment, offering a physical "reset."

Building a Sustainable Focus Practice

Transforming brain fog into brain focus isn't a one-time fix. It's about developing a set of habits and coping mechanisms you can rely on daily. The more you practice them, the more resilient your focus becomes.

1. **Consistency Over Intensity**: It's better to do 5–10 minutes of "brain hygiene" every day (like a quick brain dump or environment check) than to attempt a massive overhaul once a month.
2. **Track Your Wins**: Keep a simple log of times you successfully focused on a task. Positive reinforcement can build momentum and encourage repeat behavior.
3. **Stay Flexible**: ADHD management is all about adapting. If a tactic stops working, pivot. Reevaluate your environment, your schedule, or your mental health. Experimentation is key.

Closing Thoughts: Progress, Not Perfection

So, can you wave a magic wand and banish brain fog forever? Probably not—ADHD minds will always have a certain flair for wandering. But with intentional tools, small routine tweaks, and a dash of self-compassion, you can significantly reduce how often you feel helpless in the face of your own distractibility.

Think of your brain as an unruly but gifted companion. It can conjure incredible creativity and insight—if you learn to guide it gently rather than scolding it relentlessly. Sure, it might wander off the trail occasionally to sniff an interesting flower or chase a squirrel, but with patient training (and maybe a sturdy leash of timers and habit cues), you'll find yourself enjoying a more purposeful journey.

In the next chapter, we'll explore how to build tiny, sustainable habits that support this clarity and keep the organizing momentum going. After all, harnessing focus is only step one; *maintaining* it day after day is where the real transformation begins. Until then, remember: every time you catch yourself drifting and steer back on course, you've just done another rep in the mental gym of ADHD management. Keep lifting those focus muscles, friend—you're getting stronger with each small success.

4

The Power of (Tiny) Habits

If you've spent any amount of time on social media, you've likely seen those dramatic before-and-after videos: a cluttered room miraculously transformed into an immaculate living space in 30 seconds. It's hypnotic to watch, but here's the catch: those transformations rarely reflect the slow, steady process required in real life—especially if you're juggling ADHD. For many of us, the idea of overhauling everything at once feels like a Herculean task doomed to fail on day three, when we can't remember half the changes we attempted to implement.

Enter the concept of **tiny habits**. These small, deliberate shifts in your daily routine might not offer the instant gratification of a viral TikTok cleaning spree, but over time, they create lasting change that sticks. In this chapter, we'll explore why tiny habits are such a game-changer for ADHD minds, how to design them effectively, and how to sustain them without falling into the dreaded perfectionism pit.

Why Tiny Habits Work for ADHD

We've all had grand visions of reorganizing the entire house in a single weekend or finally committing to a color-coded scheduling system... only to fizzle out after a few days. While motivation surges can be great for short bursts, they aren't reliable for long-term transformation—especially when you have ADHD.

1. Manageable Brain Load

ADHD often comes with a delicate working memory. When you try to make ten big changes at once, it's like asking your brain's internal juggler to handle flaming torches, swords, and water balloons simultaneously. Inevitably, something gets dropped. Tiny habits reduce cognitive overload because you're only focusing on one small change at a time—like adding a two-minute stretch routine in the morning or always putting your keys on the same hook.

2. Instant Wins Fuel Dopamine

ADHD brains love instant gratification. We often chase novelty or short-term rewards because that sweet hit of dopamine feels amazing. Tiny habits tap into this by offering quick, repeatable victories. When you complete a small habit—like making your bed or jotting down a daily goal—you get a mini-boost of accomplishment that motivates you to keep going.

3. Building Momentum is Easier

Habits function like compound interest. One small shift, repeated daily, can lead to significant outcomes over time. For ADHD minds, creating momentum is crucial. Once you see small successes stacking up, you're more likely to believe you *can* build on that foundation. It's much less daunting than trying to scale the entire mountain in one leap.

Designing Tiny Habits That Stick

So how do we move from "I want to be more organized" to "I now do a quick tidy of my workspace every evening—without fail"? The secret is in the design. A well-designed tiny habit meets your ADHD brain where it's at, instead of demanding you fit a rigid blueprint that might work for someone else but leaves you frustrated.

1. Anchor New Habits to Existing Routines

One of the most effective strategies is **habit stacking**, a term popularized by author James Clear. The idea is simple: you attach a new habit to something you *already do consistently*. For example:

- **After I Brew My Morning Coffee → I Will Sort Yesterday's Mail for Two Minutes**
- **After I Finish Brushing My Teeth at Night → I Will Lay Out My Clothes for Tomorrow**

By anchoring the new habit to an existing routine, you bypass the need to remember it out of thin air. Your existing routine serves as a cue or trigger that says, "Oh right, time for my two-minute mail check."

2. Make It Ridiculously Easy

ADHD brains can rebel against tasks that feel large or tedious. By making the habit *ridiculously easy*, you remove much of the mental friction. Examples:

- **Want to start journaling?** Commit to writing *just one sentence* a day.
- **Want to tidy your workspace?** Commit to putting away *just one object* at the end of the day.

It may sound too small to matter, but it's not. In practice, you'll often exceed the bare minimum once you start. The goal is to ensure that getting started is simple enough that your ADHD brain doesn't go into "Too Hard, Didn't Do" mode.

3. Pair Habits with Positive Emotions

ADHD is heavily influenced by emotions and rewards. If you attach a positive feeling to a new habit, you're more likely to stick with it. You can do this by:

- **Celebrating Immediately**: Give yourself a mental high-five or do a little dance right after completing the habit.
- **Using a Reward**: Enjoy a piece of dark chocolate, watch a short funny video, or indulge in a favorite song after finishing your tiny habit.

- **Tracking Progress Visually**: Mark a calendar or habit tracker each day you complete the habit. Watching your streak grow feels surprisingly satisfying.

Examples of Tiny Habits for ADHD Organization

Let's brainstorm a few small habits that can have an outsized impact on your day-to-day life. Pick one (or two at most) that resonates with you and give it a whirl. Remember, keep it tiny.

Habit 1: 60-Second Desk Declutter

- **Anchor**: After you shut down your computer for the day, do this habit.
- **Tiny Task**: Spend 60 seconds putting stray papers into a folder or the recycling bin. Move cups to the kitchen, return pens to their holder, and tuck away any clutter.
- **Reward**: Admire your tidier desk, and maybe say, "Yes, Queen!" out loud for dramatic effect.

Habit 2: The "Keys on the Hook" Rule

- **Anchor**: When you walk through the door.
- **Tiny Task**: Hang your keys on the designated hook *immediately* instead of tossing them on the nearest flat surface.
- **Reward**: No more morning searches for your keys! (And you can treat yourself to a small treat if you want immediate positive reinforcement.)

Habit 3: 1-Minute Task Triage

- **Anchor**: Right after you check your phone in the morning (let's admit it: we all do).
- **Tiny Task**: Jot down your top 3 tasks for the day on a sticky note. That's it—just identify them.
- **Reward**: Take a deep breath and appreciate that you have a mini-roadmap for the day.

Habit 4: Laundry Launch Pad

- **Anchor**: After brushing your teeth in the morning or at night.
- **Tiny Task**: Put *just one load* of laundry into the washer. You don't have to fold or put away—just start the load.
- **Reward**: That smug satisfaction that you won't be running out of clean socks again (at least not this week).

By focusing on small tasks, you gradually reduce chaos in your environment, which in turn lowers your stress levels and frees up mental space.

Overcoming Common ADHD Roadblocks to Habit-Building

Even with the best intentions and perfectly designed tiny habits, ADHD can throw curveballs. Life gets hectic, motivation dips, or that initial excitement fades. Here's how to handle typical hurdles:

Roadblock 1: Forgetting Your New Habit

You promised yourself you'd do a quick tidy each day, but you keep forgetting until right before bed when you're already half-asleep. This is where **visual or auditory cues** can save the day.

- **Set Alarms or Reminders**: A simple phone alert can jog your memory.
- **Post-It Notes**: Stick them on your bathroom mirror or desk to remind you of your micro-task.
- **Pairing**: If your habit is tidying up at night, pair it with something you already do reliably, like locking the front door or turning off the TV.

Roadblock 2: Losing Interest

ADHD often thrives on novelty. Once something becomes routine, the allure can vanish, leading us back to old patterns. Combat boredom by **updating your habit** in small ways:

- **Switch Up the Environment**: If you're journaling, move from your desk to a cozy chair.
- **Change Tools**: Swap a basic notepad for a colorful notebook or a digital app with fun features.
- **Reward Upgrades**: If you've gotten bored with your initial reward (like a piece of chocolate), spice it up. Maybe watch a favorite YouTuber, treat yourself to fancy tea, or take a five-minute dance break.

Roadblock 3: All-or-Nothing Mindset

Sometimes you might miss a day (or three) and think, *"Well, that's it. I've failed."* The all-or-nothing trap is particularly potent for ADHD brains with perfectionist tendencies. The key is to adopt a more flexible view:

- **Embrace "Streak Pauses"**: If you break your streak, treat it as a temporary pause rather than a total meltdown.
- **Reflect, Don't Judge**: Ask, "Why did I miss my habit? Was it stress, forgetting, or something else?" Adjust accordingly.
- **Keep the Habit Tiny**: If you're failing because it feels too big, shrink the habit further until it's almost effortless.

Roadblock 4: Getting Overwhelmed by Too Many Habits

It's tempting to try a handful of new habits at once—especially if you're feeling extra motivated. But that can overload your ADHD brain. A simpler strategy is **one new habit at a time**. Once the first habit feels second-nature, add another. This gradual approach respects your energy and reduces the chance of burnout.

Building a Habit "Dashboard"

For those who love visual motivation, creating a habit "dashboard" can be a fun way to track progress without succumbing to overwhelm. This could be a simple chart, a bullet journal spread, or a digital app. The goal is to see at a glance how consistent you've been.

1. **List Your Tiny Habit(s)**: Keep it to one or two when starting.
2. **Date Columns**: Have a column for each day of the week or month.
3. **Mark Completions**: Check off, color in, or add a sticker when you complete the habit.
4. **Celebrate**: Notice any patterns—do you miss the habit on weekends? Are you consistently hitting your stride on Tuesdays? Use these insights to refine your approach.

Watching your completed habit marks stack up can be deeply satisfying, giving your ADHD brain that nice hit of reward chemicals. Plus, when you see you've done something for 10 or 20 days in a row, you're less likely to want to break that streak.

When Habits Evolve Into Routines

Tiny habits can act as building blocks for larger routines. Over time, separate habits can merge into a morning or evening sequence that runs almost on autopilot. For instance:

1. **Wake Up → Make Bed**
2. **Bathroom → Quick Journaling (1 Sentence)**
3. **Coffee → Sort Yesterday's Mail**
4. **Before Leaving → Keys on the Hook**

Individually, each step is minuscule. Together, they form a routine that sets the tone for a more organized day. The beauty of this approach is that it develops organically. You're not forcing yourself into a rigid schedule overnight; you're letting small habits accumulate until you have a cohesive flow.

Balancing Habit Tracking with Self-Compassion

While tracking and consistency matter, remember the lessons from previous chapters about shame and self-compassion. Your worth isn't tied to the number of habit streaks you maintain. Some days you might not manage your tiny habit because life threw you a curveball, or your brain simply refused to cooperate. That's okay.

- **Look for Patterns Over Perfection**: Consistency is the goal, but slip-ups are normal. Strive for progress, not a spotless record.
- **Reward Yourself for Trying**: Even on days you don't complete the habit, acknowledge the fact that you *intended* to do it. ADHD is often about managing intentions vs. actions. Every step forward counts, even if it's small.

Real-Life Stories: Tiny Habits in Action

Camille's Two-Minute Tidy

Camille, a busy mom with ADHD, always felt guilty about the state of her living room. Kids' toys, dog hair, and random junk mail covered every surface. She decided on a tiny habit: two minutes of tidying every night before bed. At first, it seemed laughable—how much difference could two minutes make? But by focusing on just one specific corner each night, the overall mess began to recede. Seeing a cleaner living room motivated Camille to extend her tidy sessions—often she kept going past the two-minute mark because she was already in motion.

Ana's "One Sticky Note" Work Routine

Ana struggled at her office job; her ADHD made it tough to prioritize tasks. She started writing down just one key work task on a sticky note every morning and placing it on her keyboard. Once she finished that one task, she'd write another. Over time, Ana noticed she was finishing more high-impact tasks because she wasn't overwhelmed by a giant list. That one sticky note habit evolved into a short daily planning ritual that helped her get clearer on her goals each day.

Tiny Habits for a Big-Hearted Life

At its core, habit-building isn't just about a cleaner house or a more organized planner; it's about easing the weight on your mind so you can enjoy life more fully. When you're not constantly tripping over undone chores or forgotten responsibilities, you have more emotional bandwidth for relationships, hobbies, and self-care. Tiny habits become stepping stones toward the life you genuinely want, rather than a life spent firefighting one crisis after another.

Where to Go From Here

By now, you understand the *why* and *how* of tiny habits, and you've got some ideas to experiment with. The next step is to pick just **one** and start. It might be as simple as:

- **"After I make my coffee, I will put away one item on the kitchen counter."**

Do it for a week and watch how your mindset begins to shift. You may notice less guilt about "never doing enough," and more confidence in your ability to follow through—even if it's only for a short, purposeful moment each day.

In **Chapter 5**, we'll dive into harnessing "mindset magic," exploring the journey from negative mental loops to positive pep-talks. A strong mindset will further boost the staying power of these tiny habits. But for now, celebrate the small steps you're already taking: reading this chapter, thinking about changes, and daring to believe that big transformations can start incredibly small. And remember, every time you do that tiny habit—even if it feels inconsequential—you're building evidence that you *can* create an organized, manageable life on your own terms.

5

Mindset Magic—From Negative Loops to Positive Pep-Talks

You're standing at the kitchen counter, staring at the mountain of unopened mail, random receipts, and bits of snack wrappers that mysteriously accumulate (often overnight). Your first thought: *"Ugh, I'm such a mess. Why can't I get it together?"* If this refrain sounds familiar, you're far from alone. Many of us with ADHD know all too well the mental soundtrack that repeats variations of *not good enough, disorganized, lazy, or hopeless* from sunrise to sunset.

Welcome to the realm of **negative loops**: automatic, critical thoughts that replay in your mind like a broken record, undermining your confidence and draining your motivation. The good news? You don't have to accept these loops as reality. By learning to spot, challenge, and transform them, you open a door to a kinder, more supportive internal dialogue. Think of it as upgrading from a sarcastic drill sergeant to a wise, encouraging friend—someone who reminds you of your strengths even when you're elbow-deep in junk mail.

The ADHD Brain on Negative Loops

Negative thinking isn't unique to ADHD, but certain traits of ADHD can magnify its impact. When your brain already struggles with impulsivity or emotional regulation, a single negative thought can quickly spiral into a full-blown mental drama. One slip-up—like being late for an appointment—can trigger an avalanche of self-criticism about everything from your daily habits to your life choices.

Emotional Reactivity

ADHD often involves intense emotional reactions. Imagine you're slightly frustrated by something minor—like misplacing your keys—then *bam!* That small frustration morphs into a wave of shame or anger. In that heightened emotional state, negative thoughts gain extra traction.

All-or-Nothing Mindset

Many women with ADHD see tasks in extremes. You're either hyper-focused, doing them perfectly, or you feel you're failing miserably. When you don't achieve 100%, your inner critic can rush in to declare, *"You messed up again. Typical!"* This black-and-white perspective fuels negative loops that ignore the nuances and progress in between.

Rejection Sensitivity

If you're sensitive to perceived rejection or criticism (a common aspect of ADHD called Rejection Sensitive Dysphoria), negative feedback can cut deeper. Even well-intentioned advice from a friend can spark a harsh internal monologue: *"They think I'm lazy. I should've done better. I'm worthless."* Over time, these emotional flare-ups create a "mental file" of negativity that's too easy to access.

How Negative Loops Form—and Why They Stick

Negative loops typically form when your brain repeatedly pairs a certain situation (like a messy home or a missed deadline) with a harsh self-judgment. Over time, these pairings become ingrained, so that the second you notice a messy home, the self-judgment automatically follows.

Childhood Conditioning and Social Pressures

Many women with ADHD grew up hearing some version of *"Pay attention," "You're so disorganized," "Why are you so forgetful?"* This persistent feedback can become internalized. By adulthood, you might not need external voices; you've internalized the criticism so well that you criticize yourself automatically.

Self-Preservation... Gone Awry

In a twisted way, negative loops can feel like *protection.* The idea is: if you criticize yourself first, it won't sting as badly if someone else does it. While this might seem logical in the short term, it quickly becomes self-sabotaging—eroding your self-esteem and draining your energy.

Confirmation Bias

Your brain loves to confirm what it already believes. If you hold a core belief like *"I'm never organized,"* you'll zero in on every instance that seems to validate that belief, ignoring counterexamples (like the times you did manage tasks effectively). This mental bias makes it challenging to break free from negative loops—unless you actively decide to shift gears.

Spotting and Interrupting the Loop

The first step in changing your internal narrative is recognizing when you've entered a negative spiral. Often, the signs are physical and emotional before you even notice the thoughts:

1. **Physical Tension**: Do you clench your jaw or hunch your shoulders? Does your heart rate pick up?
2. **Mood Dip**: Suddenly, you feel deflated, sad, or angry—even if the trigger seems small.
3. **Harsh Internal Commentary**: The words "never," "always," or "why can't I" might start floating through your thoughts.

Once you spot these signs, **pause**. Take a deep breath or two, and mentally label what's happening: "I'm having one of those negative loops again." This labeling alone can provide a small but powerful buffer between you and the automatic pattern.

From Critic to Coach: Rewriting Your Self-Talk

Changing your self-talk doesn't mean simply ignoring your faults or wrapping yourself in empty affirmations. It means shifting from a punitive mindset to a *constructive* one. Instead of, *"I can't believe I forgot that again. I'm so scatterbrained!"* you try, *"I forgot. It happens. How can I set a reminder for next time?"*

A 3-Step Reframe

1. **Identify the Negative Thought**

- Example: "I'm such a mess."

1. **Challenge Its Accuracy**

- Ask: "Is this 100% true? Are there times I'm actually quite put-together?"
- Usually, reality is more nuanced. Sometimes you are messy, but sometimes you're quite capable of being organized—like when you planned that birthday party flawlessly.

1. **Rewrite in a Supportive Tone**

- Replace the original statement with something that acknowledges the problem but focuses on growth: "I'm feeling overwhelmed right now. I can take a small step to tidy up, or find a system that works better for me."

This might feel awkward at first, especially if you're used to a steady diet of self-criticism. Over time, though, you'll discover that supportive self-talk leads to more productive actions and less emotional fallout.

The Power of a Growth Mindset

In previous chapters, we've touched on perfectionism—how it traps you into believing you're either 100% successful or a complete disaster. That's a classic **fixed mindset**, where your abilities (and flaws) are seen as set in stone. A **growth mindset**, on the other hand, encourages you to see challenges and setbacks as opportunities to learn and improve.

How It Looks in Real Life

- **Fixed Mindset**: "I'm terrible at managing money. It's just who I am."
- **Growth Mindset**: "I've struggled with budgeting in the past, but I can learn new skills and tools to get better."

When you adopt a growth mindset, each misstep becomes part of the learning curve, rather than a personal indictment of your worth.

Using Tools and Techniques to Stay Positive

While rewriting your self-talk is the core practice, a few strategies can make the journey easier. Think of them as scaffolding that supports your evolving mindset until it becomes more natural.

1. Affirmation Cards or Sticky Notes

Write encouraging messages to yourself on cards or sticky notes. For instance:

- "My ADHD brain can be messy, but it's also creative and adaptable."
- "Done is better than perfect. One small step is progress."

Place them where you'll see them daily—on your bathroom mirror, computer monitor, or fridge. Over time, these cues can replace negative loops with gentler, more optimistic statements.

2. Journaling with a Twist

Instead of a standard diary, try a **reframe journal**:

1. **Situation**: Describe what happened (e.g., left the stove on again).
2. **Initial Thought**: Write down the negative self-talk that popped up (e.g., "I'm so irresponsible!").
3. **Reframe**: Challenge and replace it (e.g., "I'm capable of remembering important things. Next time, I'll set a phone alert to double-check before leaving the house.").

Reflecting on these entries over time helps you track progress in how you speak to yourself.

3. Community and Accountability

Having a friend or coach who understands ADHD can provide an external voice of reason. If you catch yourself spiraling, reach out. You might say, "I'm stuck in negative thoughts—can you help me reframe?" This outside perspective often sees your strengths more clearly than you do in that moment of self-doubt.

4. Incorporating Mindfulness

We touched on mindfulness techniques in Chapter 3. Practices like meditation, deep breathing, or even mindful walking can ground you in the present moment. The calmer your mind, the easier it is to notice and challenge negative loops before they become full-blown emotional storms.

Real Stories: Overcoming the Negative Narrative

Story 1: Marisol's Sticky Note Strategies

Marisol, a busy paralegal with ADHD, constantly told herself she was "terrible at details." After multiple slip-ups at work, she started leaving sticky notes on her computer monitor with simple statements: "I'm capable. I'm learning systems that work for me." Initially, it felt cheesy, but those daily reminders gradually replaced the mental tape of *I always mess up.* When she did inevitably slip, she'd focus on improving her systems (like color-coded checklists) rather than berating herself.

Story 2: Leah's "3 Wins" Journal

Leah found that by 9 p.m., her brain was replaying every mistake from the day—forgetting an email, messing up dinner plans, etc. To combat this, she adopted a simple journal practice: before bed, she wrote down three things she did *well* that day, no matter how small. It might be as simple as *I returned a friend's call on time,* or *I cleared one corner of my desk.* Over a month, Leah noticed her negative loops softened as she realized each day had at least a few wins, proving she wasn't the hopeless mess her inner critic claimed.

Practice, Patience, and Progress

Transforming negative loops into positive pep-talks is like learning a new language—your brain's default might still be negativity, especially under stress. But each time you actively reframe a harsh thought, you strengthen the neural pathways for a gentler, growth-oriented mindset.

Accepting Imperfection

Even with regular practice, you'll have days when old patterns take over. Maybe you're exhausted, the kids are screaming, or you're late on a work deadline, and your self-talk reverts to *"I can't do anything right!"* That's normal. Forgive the slip, and when you can, make a conscious effort to reframe again: *"This is a rough moment, not a reflection of my entire identity."*

Celebrating Incremental Changes

Over time, you may notice that negative loops arise less frequently or lose their intensity. Perhaps you used to berate yourself for losing your keys five times a week, but now it's only once or twice, and you catch it sooner. Those are signs of genuine progress—worth celebrating just as you would any other milestone in your ADHD organization journey.

Linking Mindset to Action

Rewiring your mindset doesn't mean ignoring practical systems (like habit-stacking and environment optimization). In fact, they reinforce each other. A more positive internal dialogue makes you *more* likely to try new organizational strategies without fear of failure. Meanwhile, each small success in creating an organized space or nailing a tiny habit feeds back into a more confident mindset.

1. **Positive Mindset → Courage to Experiment**

- You'll dare to try a new planner or organizational app because you're no longer telling yourself you'll fail instantly.

1. **Practical Results → Boost in Self-Esteem**

- When you see even modest wins—like remembering to sort mail daily—you have tangible evidence that you *can* improve, reinforcing your supportive self-talk.

Moving Forward with a Brighter Inner Voice

Imagine waking up tomorrow and greeting your day with, *"I'm learning to navigate my ADHD one step at a time, and that's enough."* Instead of harshly criticizing yourself for every slip, you gently course-correct. Over weeks and months, that shift can reshape your entire life experience. You'll likely still misplace the occasional sock or forget an errand here and there—that's part of being human. But with a kinder inner voice, those moments become opportunities to adjust, rather than reasons to spiral.

Action Steps

- **Monitor Your Thoughts**: For the next week, pick one day to be especially mindful of negative self-talk. Use a note on your phone or a small notebook to jot them down. Then, practice reframing at least one each day.
- **Use a Visual Cue**: Post a phrase like "Speak to yourself like you would to a dear friend" in a place you frequently look. This reminds you to keep an eye on your internal language.
- **Team Up**: Find a friend or accountability buddy on the same journey. Agree to gently call each other out when you hear negative loops. Support each other with encouraging reframes.

Remember, your mind is the control center for all the organizational strategies you're learning. When it's locked in a cycle of self-condemnation, you end up exhausted before you've even begun. By nurturing a supportive, optimistic inner dialogue, you free up mental and emotional energy to implement all the tools—tiny habits, time management hacks, environment tweaks—that truly help you thrive.

6

Dealing with Decision Paralysis

It's Thursday morning. You're standing in front of your closet, mentally wading through a sea of shirts, sweaters, skirts, and dresses. Nothing seems right, so you check the weather, only to find that it's "unseasonably warm," which derails the sweater idea. Suddenly, choosing what to wear for the day feels like solving a complex equation—and the rest of your morning routine comes to a grinding halt. If you've ever felt that *deciding* is sometimes harder than *doing*, welcome to the world of **decision paralysis**.

Many adults with ADHD struggle with decision-making. It's not laziness or lack of interest, but rather a mental jam where too many options, too many uncertainties, or too few cues for what's "right" send your brain into meltdown mode. The stakes can be as small as picking an outfit or as big as choosing a career path. Either way, that swirling sense of overwhelm can stall progress, derail productivity, and spark a whole lot of second-guessing.

In this chapter, we'll explore the *why* behind decision paralysis, and more importantly, share practical strategies to unstick yourself. By the end, you'll have tools to make choices—big or small—with more clarity and less drama.

The Anatomy of ADHD Decision Paralysis

On paper, decision-making seems straightforward: identify the problem, consider possible solutions, pick one. Easy-peasy, right? Except the ADHD mind rarely follows that neat linear path. Instead, it's more like:

1. **Spot the Problem:** "I need to decide on a project topic at work."
2. **Tornado of Ideas:** Your brain conjures 47 possible angles, each with its own pros and cons.
3. **Overwhelm Takes Over:** Suddenly, picking any single option feels like a major risk, so you second-guess everything.
4. **Stalemate:** You do nothing, or you flip-flop between ideas until the last possible second.

Working Memory Woes

Executive function challenges in ADHD often mean keeping multiple variables in mind at once is harder. The more complex the decision—like a multi-step project plan—the more likely you are to lose track of key details or shift focus halfway through.

Emotional Overload

When you hit a decision snag, anxiety, perfectionism, and fear of failure can pile on. The result? A mental soup of *"What if I pick the wrong thing?"* that further clouds your ability to choose confidently.

Choice Fatigue

As a woman with ADHD, you might be juggling job responsibilities, family schedules, social commitments, and personal errands. Each domain requires countless micro-decisions. Over time, you can burn out simply from deciding too many things in a day—leading to impulsive or avoidant behaviors for the next decision that pops up.

Why Decision Paralysis Feels So Much Worse for Women

Women often bear a heavy **mental load**, overseeing everything from meal planning to remembering Aunt Susan's birthday. Coupled with societal expectations to "have it all together," the pressure can escalate. The sense that "everyone is counting on me" amplifies normal decision-making stress into a pressure cooker.

- **Household Management**: Even if chores are theoretically shared, many women end up as the "manager" of the household—deciding which groceries to buy, what appointments need scheduling, what items need restocking.
- **Emotional Labor**: Anticipating others' needs (like a partner's preference for dinner or a child's upcoming school project) adds layers of complexity to everyday decisions.
- **ADHD Masking**: Feeling the need to appear organized and capable can make decisions more fraught. You might obsess over the "perfect" choice instead of a "good enough" one, fearing judgment or criticism.

Recognizing these extra layers of expectation and emotional labor is the first step in breaking free from paralysis. It's not that you're "bad at deciding"; you're simply juggling more variables than your executive function can handle smoothly.

Strategy 1: Simplify Your Options

When you have a swirl of ideas in your head, the first task is to trim them down. Fewer choices often mean quicker, easier decisions.

The "Rule of Three"

Limit yourself to **three** possible options. Whether it's picking a lunch spot, deciding on a weekend activity, or choosing a new job opportunity, forcing yourself to consider only three choices narrows the field:

1. **Brainstorm Freely**: Jot down every possibility.
2. **Evaluate Quickly**: Cross out duplicates or obvious duds.
3. **Pick Your Top Three**: Trust your gut here—ask, "Which three feel most viable or interesting?"

Next, focus solely on these three. Let the rest fade into the background. When your ADHD mind tries to reintroduce more options, gently remind yourself you're on a "three-choice limit."

Pre-Decided Defaults

For recurring decisions (like what to make for dinner on Wednesdays or which brand of laundry detergent to buy), create **default choices**. For example:

- **Taco Tuesday**: Instead of scanning 100 recipe ideas, default to making tacos every Tuesday.
- **Favorite Detergent**: Stick with one brand you like, so you don't get stuck in the laundry aisle debating scents.

Defaults free up mental real estate. You can always deviate if you're feeling adventurous, but the default baseline prevents you from having to reinvent the wheel each time.

Strategy 2: Break Big Decisions into Micro-Choices

Complex decisions, like planning a large project or reorganizing your home office, can be paralyzing because they involve multiple steps. Rather than deciding everything at once, break it down into a series of smaller, sequential choices.

1. **Identify the End Goal**: "I want a functional home office."
2. **List Sub-Decisions**:

- Which corner of the room to use for the desk?
- What type of desk/chair setup do I want?
- Do I need extra storage?
- Will I paint the walls or buy décor?

1. **Tackle One Sub-Decision at a Time**: Resist the urge to do

them all simultaneously. Start with the desk placement, for instance, and only after that's finalized, move on to the next.

By focusing on bite-sized decisions, your working memory and emotional bandwidth are less likely to get overwhelmed. Plus, each small success builds momentum, reducing the stress around the next choice.

Strategy 3: Impose Time Limits

ADHD can cause time distortion—you might hyperfocus and spend hours researching options, or you might procrastinate until a deadline forces a frantic choice. Setting a reasonable yet firm time constraint can keep you from drifting into endless indecision.

The Timer Trick

- **Set a Timer for Research**: Decide you'll spend exactly 20 minutes gathering info about something (like a travel destination or new laptop). When the timer rings, stop researching.
- **Block Off Decision Time**: Allocate another set period—say 10 minutes—to review what you found and pick your top contender.

If you feel anxious about "not knowing enough," remind yourself that perfect knowledge is unattainable anyway. What you gather in a focused session is usually sufficient for a good decision. And in many cases, a "good enough" decision made on time beats a theoretically perfect choice made too late.

Strategy 4: Use Visual Decision Tools

When your mind is swirling with details, seeing those details externally can bring clarity. Visual tools also engage your brain differently—turning abstract thoughts into something tangible and organized.

The Basic Pros and Cons List

It sounds cliché, but writing a simple pros and cons list helps your ADHD mind structure information. Make it more ADHD-friendly by:

- **Adding a Third Column**: "Mitigations." If a con is "Expensive," a possible mitigation might be "Find a discount" or "Buy used." This addition reminds you that some downsides can be addressed rather than disqualifying the entire option.
- **Color Coding**: Highlight especially compelling pros or severe cons in different colors. Visual cues can help you quickly scan the document rather than re-reading everything.

Mind Mapping

For creative or complex decisions—like planning a party or choosing a new hobby—**mind mapping** can be a game-changer. Start with the central idea in the middle of the page. Branch out with sub-ideas, and keep branching until you've visually captured the scope. Seeing it all in a non-linear format can spark clearer insights than a standard list.

Strategy 5: Embrace "Good Enough" and Iteration

A massive hurdle for many ADHD women is perfectionism. If you believe there's exactly one "right" choice, the pressure to find it can be paralyzing. The truth? Most decisions have multiple viable paths, each with its own trade-offs.

The 80% Rule

Strive for a solution that feels 80% "right." That's typically enough to move forward effectively. If you wait for 100%, you might wait forever—or stress yourself into a meltdown.

Iterative Choices

Remember, many decisions aren't forever. You can make a choice, see how it works, and then refine or pivot. For instance, if you choose a new budgeting app and it's not a perfect fit, you can switch after a month. This iterative mindset takes the pressure off any single decision, making you more willing to choose and move on.

Strategy 6: Check In with Emotions, Not Just Logic

Women with ADHD often juggle intense emotions alongside an analytical mind. Ignoring your emotional cues can backfire, because the emotional brain will eventually revolt—or sabotage your best-laid plans. Instead, blend logic with gut checks.

The Emotion-Logic Balance

- **Data Gathering**: Use rational tools like research, lists, or mind maps.
- **Emotion Check**: Ask yourself, "Which option excites me? Which one feels draining or uneasy?"
- **Integration**: If logic points to Option A, but your gut screams Option B, see if there's a middle path. Or explore why B feels more appealing—maybe it aligns better with your values or mental health needs.

Consult Trusted Allies

Sometimes, you need an outside opinion to clarify your emotional reaction. Talk it through with a friend, therapist, or ADHD coach. A supportive listener can mirror back what they hear, helping you untangle logical concerns from emotional ones.

Strategy 7: Practice Self-Compassion During (and After) Decisions

When decisions feel overwhelming, it's easy to slip into self-blame. "I'm so indecisive. I can't handle normal adult tasks." That negative loop (as we explored in Chapter 5) only deepens paralysis. Instead, cultivate self-compassion throughout the process.

1. **Acknowledge the Challenge**: Remind yourself, "Decisions are tough for me, and that's okay. I'm learning new strategies."
2. **Celebrate Mini-Wins**: Even if you just narrow down your

options from ten to three, that's progress. Give yourself a mental high-five.
3. **Debrief Kindly**: After making a choice, avoid harsh self-criticism if the outcome isn't perfect. Ask, "What did I learn, and how can I adjust?" That's a growth mindset in action.

Real-Life Examples: Women Conquering Decision Paralysis

Example 1: Nina's "Two-Outfit Rule"

Nina dreaded morning decisions about what to wear. She'd lose 15 minutes every day trying on outfit after outfit. So she instituted a tiny system:

1. **Choose Two Outfits**: Each night, she'd pick two ensembles for the next day—both weather-appropriate and comfortable.
2. **Morning Quick Choice**: In the morning, she'd let her mood decide between the two. No third options allowed.

By limiting herself to two outfits, she cut down decision time drastically. This consistency removed morning stress, and she found she actually enjoyed her clothes more without the internal debate.

Example 2: Tasha's Brain Dump and Deadline

Tasha, a graphic designer, struggled to decide which client projects to prioritize each week. Every Monday, she did a **15-minute brain dump** of all her tasks. Then she gave herself a **5-**

minute window to pick her top three priorities—no rethinking allowed. She set an alarm on her phone, and when it buzzed, she had to finalize her three. Over time, this technique helped Tasha realize that even if she didn't pick the "perfect" top three, having *some* order was infinitely better than paralyzing indecision.

Embrace the Learning Curve

Overcoming decision paralysis doesn't happen overnight. It's a skill you build—just like any other organizational strategy. You'll experiment, stumble, refine, and grow. Some days, you might slip back into old patterns of indecision, but each time you apply these tools, you reinforce a new, more empowered way of choosing.

Reflect and Adjust

After a day or a week of using a specific strategy (like the timer trick or the pros/cons list), pause to see how it went:

- **What worked smoothly?**
- **Where did you get stuck or frustrated?**
- **Is there a tweak you could make next time?**

By regularly reflecting, you're giving your ADHD brain valuable feedback to iterate on.

The Bigger Picture: From Paralysis to Purpose

When you consistently apply strategies to beat decision paralysis, something remarkable happens: you reclaim *agency* over your life. Instead of being trapped by a spinning mind, you can move forward—whether that's organizing your closet, launching a business idea, or finally booking that long-overdue vacation.

This new sense of decisiveness spills into all areas of your day, creating a ripple effect of productivity and confidence. You might notice you procrastinate less or feel less anxious overall. That's because each decision you make underscores a subtle yet powerful message: *I'm capable of handling my life's choices.*

Action Steps to Start Right Now

1. **Pick One Repetitive Decision**: Identify a recurring decision that bogs you down—meals, outfits, bedtime routine, whatever. Create a default or limit your choices to two or three.
2. **Set Up a Decision Time Block**: Commit to using a short, focused time to decide on something you've been avoiding—like a home improvement project or a family vacation plan.
3. **Share Your Decision**: Announce your choice to a friend or family member. Sometimes, externalizing your decision helps solidify it and reduces waffling.

Remember, *done is better than perfect.* By taking a proactive stance, you're training your brain to handle decisions more smoothly. Over time, you'll realize that each choice, even if not flawless, is a step forward—learning more about your preferences, your strengths, and your ability to adapt.

7

Procrastination Rehab 101

The cat is hungry, the sink is overflowing with dishes, and your big work deadline is tomorrow. Instead of tackling any of these pressing tasks, you suddenly find yourself Googling whether penguins have knees (they do, sort of). If you've ever done everything except the thing you really need to do, you're in good company. **Procrastination** is notorious among adults with ADHD, and it's rarely about "just being lazy." Instead, it's rooted in how our brains respond to tasks, rewards, and time pressure—especially when anxiety and overwhelm start piling on.

In this chapter, we'll demystify why procrastination feels so compelling, highlight the unique twists it takes for women with ADHD, and walk through a toolbox of strategies to gently coax yourself into motion. Consider this your personal rehab plan, not from substances, but from the seductive allure of *"I'll do it later."*

Why ADHD and Procrastination Are So Intertwined

Procrastination is a universal human habit, but the ADHD brain experiences it in high definition. Our executive functions—responsible for planning, initiation, and self-regulation—tend to lag behind our best intentions. Mix in a penchant for seeking novelty (hello, random internet searches) and a tendency toward time-blindness, and you get a potent recipe for *"not now, maybe later."*

1. The Dopamine Dilemma

ADHD brains often crave immediate gratification. Tasks with a delayed payoff (like writing a lengthy report that won't be praised until next week's meeting) can feel uninspiring or even painful. We often prefer activities that yield a faster dopamine hit—like scrolling social media or rearranging our bookshelf by color.

2. Emotional Overwhelm

Tasks that appear large, vague, or high-stakes can trigger a wave of anxiety. Rather than facing that discomfort, we sidestep it by doing something—*anything*—else. Paradoxically, delaying the task often amplifies anxiety in the long run, but in the heat of the moment, avoidance seems like relief.

3. Time Blindness

ADHD minds can struggle with a slippery sense of time—everything is either "now" or "not now." A deadline a week away might as well be a year away, until it suddenly becomes *today*. This leads to the infamous cycle of last-minute scrambles, all-nighters, or missed deadlines that feed a sense of shame and failure.

4. The Fear Factor

Fear of failure or perfectionism can paralyze us. If we can't do the task perfectly—or if we fear discovering we're "not good enough"—we avoid starting altogether. It's easier to blame lack of time or last-minute chaos than confront the possibility that our best effort might fall short.

How Procrastination Manifests for Women with ADHD

While procrastination isn't exclusive to women, gender roles and societal expectations can color how it appears and how we internalize it.

1. **Invisible Work Overload**: Beyond official job duties, many women manage a hidden list of tasks—childcare logistics, household chores, emotional support for friends and family. Delaying any one item can cause a domino effect of guilt and shame.
2. **People-Pleasing Tendencies**: Some women overcommit because they fear disappointing others, then procrastinate on tasks they never had the bandwidth for in the first place.

3. **Self-Judgment Spirals**: Because we're expected (or expect ourselves) to keep everything running smoothly, procrastination can trigger severe self-criticism—*"I'm failing at being a responsible adult."*

Understanding these added pressures can help you practice more self-compassion when you inevitably find yourself organizing the spice cabinet instead of finishing that spreadsheet.

Strategy 1: Chunk Tasks into Micro-Steps

When a task looms large, your ADHD brain might scream, *"Too big, too scary!"* So, it's no surprise that you'd rather scroll for penguin facts than start. Breaking tasks into **smaller, doable chunks** can help you jump the first hurdle.

How to Chunk Effectively

1. **Define the End Goal**: For instance, "Complete my taxes."
2. **Create Micro-Steps**:

- Gather last year's documents.
- Find the W-2 forms.
- Open the tax software or website.
- Complete one section (e.g., personal info).

1. **Set Tiny Milestones**: Give yourself micro-rewards for each step—like playing your favorite upbeat song or sipping a special tea.

By focusing on the next **immediate** action instead of the entire mammoth task, you reduce overwhelm and give your brain a quick sense of achievement.

Strategy 2: Embrace the Pomodoro (or Adapt It)

The classic Pomodoro Technique involves working in 25-minute sprints followed by a short break. While it's a beloved strategy worldwide, ADHD brains often do better with adaptations to suit varying attention spans.

1. **Shorten the Sprint**: Instead of 25 minutes, try 10 or 15 if 25 feels too long.
2. **Set an Intention**: Before each sprint, decide *exactly* what you'll accomplish, like "I'll write two paragraphs of my report."
3. **Physical Reminders**: Use a visual timer (like a ticking clock app or a kitchen timer) to anchor you in the moment. ADHDers often benefit from seeing time pass.
4. **Reward After Each Sprint**: During your break, do something enjoyable—stretch, browse your phone for a few minutes (with a timer!), or pet the cat.

If standard Pomodoro cycles aren't your jam, tweak them. Some people thrive on a 40-minute focus session, others prefer 15. The key is to define your focus interval *before* you start, so you have a clear boundary for work and rest.

Strategy 3: The Power of the First Five Minutes

Often the hardest part of any task is simply beginning. Once you're past that initial resistance, momentum can carry you through. That's why focusing on the first five minutes can be a game-changer.

The 5-Minute Rule

1. **Commit**: Tell yourself you'll work on the task for just five minutes—no more.
2. **Set a Timer**: Physically set your phone or another device for five minutes.
3. **Go**: Start the task. When the alarm sounds, you're free to stop if you want.

More often than not, you'll keep going because you've already invested mental energy getting started. The brain has a sneaky way of thinking, *"Well, I've come this far—I might as well do a bit more."* But even if you stop after five minutes, you've made progress, which feels infinitely better than zero progress.

Strategy 4: External Accountability and Body Doubling

ADHD brains sometimes need an external nudge or presence to stay on track. If you've ever noticed how you can complete tasks more easily when someone else is around—even if they're not actively helping—you've experienced the **"body double"** effect.

Types of Accountability

1. **Buddy System**: Ask a friend or family member to work (or co-work) alongside you. You don't even need to be doing the same task; just having them physically (or virtually) present can anchor your focus.
2. **Support Groups**: Online forums or local ADHD meet-ups often host virtual "work sprints," where everyone logs on, states their goal, mutes themselves to work, and then checks in after a set time.
3. **Professional Help**: An ADHD coach or therapist can provide structure, set milestones, and help you reflect on your progress—or your stumbling blocks.

The presence of another person—whether in-person or virtual—can boost dopamine and keep you accountable, making procrastination less tempting.

Strategy 5: Motivational Pairing and Gamification

For many with ADHD, *motivation* isn't a steady, on-demand resource. We need novelty, excitement, or immediate pleasure to keep going. So pairing your task with something enjoyable— or turning it into a game—can jumpstart action.

Ideas for Gamification

- **Create a Points System**: Earn points for each completed sub-task; trade points for small treats (chocolate, a new book, or an hour of guilt-free TV).
- **Beat the Clock**: Challenge yourself to finish a task before a

music playlist ends or before the timer hits zero.
- **Competitive Element**: If you have a friend also looking to beat procrastination, compete on who can complete more micro-tasks in a set timeframe.

Music, Podcasts, or Rewards

Some ADHD brains focus better with background noise. Try pairing a mundane chore (like folding laundry) with an engaging podcast or an audiobook. If you're working on a more cognitively demanding task, consider instrumental music to reduce lyric-based distractions. Aligning a less exciting task with something you genuinely enjoy can transform it from a slog to at least semi-pleasant.

Strategy 6: Tame the Emotional Triggers

Procrastination often hinges on **emotional** barriers—fear of failure, perfectionism, or dread of a boring task. Handling the emotional aspect can deflate that barrier, making it easier to get started.

1. **Self-Compassion Check**: Pause and ask, "What am I feeling about this task?" Validate that feeling without shaming yourself.
2. **Reframe the Stakes**: If you're caught in catastrophic thinking (e.g., "If I don't do this perfectly, I'll lose my job!"), remind yourself that rarely is one task *that* all-or-nothing.
3. **Plan for Imperfection**: Give yourself permission to do a "rough draft" or a "messy first attempt." That lowers the

pressure, making it easier to dive in.

The Emotional Flood

If you find yourself in a full-blown emotional flood—racing heart, sweaty palms, sense of doom—try a grounding technique:

- **Box Breathing**: Inhale for a count of four, hold for four, exhale for four, and hold for four.
- **5-4-3-2-1**: Name 5 things you see, 4 you can touch, 3 you can hear, 2 you can smell, and 1 you can taste (or simply like).

Calming your nervous system helps your rational mind regain control, making procrastination less "necessary" as an emotional escape.

Strategy 7: Forgive Yourself and Course-Correct

Let's be real: you *will* procrastinate again. You're human, and you're also working with an ADHD brain that thrives on novelty and struggles with boring tasks. The crucial difference is learning to handle those lapses *without* spiraling into shame or self-punishment.

The Shame Spiral vs. Productive Reflection

- **Shame Spiral**: "I did it again. I'm hopeless. I'll never learn."
- **Productive Reflection**: "I got stuck. Why? Was it the environment, a lack of clarity, or emotional overwhelm? How can I adjust next time?"

When you respond to slip-ups with curiosity rather than condemnation, you shift from paralyzing guilt to constructive planning. This fosters a growth mindset where every procrastination episode becomes an opportunity to refine your strategies.

Real-Life Story: Carmen's 2-Minute Desk Strategy

Carmen, a freelance writer, frequently found herself browsing random articles instead of tackling her assignments. The looming deadlines only increased her anxiety, which made her procrastinate more. Fed up, she adopted a **2-Minute Desk Strategy**:

1. **Name the Task**: "Write the introduction to my article."
2. **Set a 2-Minute Timer**: She opened her document and gave herself permission to stop after two minutes of writing.
3. **Follow the Momentum**: More often than not, she continued working past the timer, because she was already "in the zone."

When she did stop, she reframed it as a tiny victory: *"I wrote for two solid minutes; that's better than zero."* Over time, the habit stuck, and her articles got written with less last-minute panic.

Putting It All Together: Your Personal Procrastination Rehab Plan

You don't need every strategy to break free from procrastination. Pick a few that resonate—ones that feel **easy** or **exciting** to implement. Experiment for a week or two, observe what happens, and course-correct as needed.

1. **Identify a Trigger Task**: Something you consistently delay (bills, returning emails, cleaning the bathroom—take your pick).
2. **Choose One or Two Strategies**: Maybe you try the **First Five Minutes** rule paired with a **Buddy System**.
3. **Track Progress**: Keep it simple—a tally on a Post-it note or a quick digital log. How often did you avoid the task vs. actually do it?
4. **Reward Small Wins**: Each time you succeed in starting or finishing the task, celebrate. Text a friend, treat yourself to a fun snack, or blast your favorite pump-up song.
5. **Reflect Weekly**: Check in with yourself. Did these strategies reduce your procrastination? If yes, keep going. If not, swap in a different approach from the toolbox.

A Note on Professional Support

If procrastination is severely impacting your job, relationships, or self-esteem, consider professional help. An ADHD coach or therapist can:

- **Provide Accountability**: Regular check-ins on your progress.

- **Refine Strategies**: Tailor techniques to your unique challenges.
- **Offer Emotional Support**: Help address deeper fears, shame, or traumatic experiences tied to chronic procrastination.

Medication, when prescribed by a qualified professional, can also help regulate attention and motivation, making it easier to employ these strategies effectively.

Beyond Procrastination: Reclaiming Your Momentum

When you start to break the procrastination cycle, you reclaim time and mental space you didn't realize you were missing. Tasks become less daunting, and you free yourself to focus on what truly matters—whether that's building a creative side hustle, spending quality time with loved ones, or simply relaxing without a cloud of *unstarted projects* hovering overhead.

Progress, however, isn't linear. You'll have days (or weeks) where you slip back into old habits. That's normal—especially with ADHD. The key is recognizing the pattern sooner, using your rehab tools to pivot, and moving forward with self-compassion.

Closing Thoughts

Procrastination is less about laziness and more about the delicate dance between your ADHD wiring, emotional triggers, and environmental cues. By chunking tasks, leveraging accountability, and managing emotional drivers, you can transform "I'll do it later" into "Hey, I'm already doing it now!" Even if you only manage five or ten minutes at a time, you'll discover a new sense of control—and relief—as those micro-moments of productivity start adding up.

8

Who Moved My Keys? Mindful Organization for Women With Squirrels in the Brain

One minute you're standing by the front door, keys in hand, ready to head out. The next, you're rummaging under couch cushions, checking the junk drawer, and interrogating the cat, because somewhere in that brief moment, your keys vanished. Sound familiar? If you've ever felt like you're constantly playing an unintentional game of hide-and-seek with your own belongings, you're not alone. This is the reality for many women with ADHD, where disorganization and forgetfulness collide in a daily "Where did I put that?" marathon.

You've tackled procrastination, decision paralysis, and negative self-talk. Now it's time to explore a gentler, more holistic approach to organizing your life: **mindfulness**. Think of mindfulness not as a lofty, incense-filled spiritual practice (though incense is optional) but rather as the art of being fully present in your daily routines—especially those that tend to slip through the cracks of a busy, ADHD-addled mind. By weaving mindfulness into how you store items, manage routines, and handle everyday tasks, you can reduce the frantic searches and free up mental space for the things that truly matter.

The Link Between Mindfulness and Organization

Mindfulness at its core is about paying attention *on purpose*. When you're mindful, you notice where you place your keys instead of absentmindedly tossing them onto the nearest surface. You remember to take a quick breath before diving into your closet to find an outfit, rather than letting your swirling thoughts push you into a flurry of rummaging.

ADHD vs. Autopilot

We often go on autopilot during mundane tasks. This autopilot mode can be even stronger for ADHD brains craving novelty—why bother paying attention to routine tasks when you can daydream about your latest hobby or replay that funny TV show scene in your head? Yet it's precisely during these "boring" moments when mindfulness can save you time, energy, and frustration.

- **Autopilot Example**: You come home, fling your keys and mail onto a random surface, and dash to the bathroom or the kitchen. Later, you have no idea where your keys ended up.
- **Mindful Example**: You come home and pause briefly. You notice the weight of the keys in your hand. You take a step toward your designated key hook (or dish), place the keys there, and *feel* your hand let go of them.

It sounds trivial, but those few seconds can make the difference between a relaxed departure and a last-minute frantic hunt.

Strategy 1: Create "Mindful Landing Pads"

When everything in your home lacks a designated place, items float around until they end up wherever you happen to drop them. By creating **mindful landing pads**—specific spots for frequently-used items—you'll train yourself to place things down *with intention.*

Step-by-Step Landing Pad Setup

1. **Identify Your Hot Spots**: Where does clutter pile up, and which items go missing most frequently? Common culprits might include keys, wallets, headphones, mail, or sunglasses.
2. **Designate a Visible, Accessible Space**: Put a hook or small tray near your front door for keys. Keep a small basket on your desk for earbuds. Choose a spot for your mail that you naturally pass by when you come home.
3. **Make It Appealing**: If you're visually drawn to your landing pad, you're more likely to use it. Pick trays or bowls in colors or patterns you love. Attach a quirky keychain to your keys that makes you smile when you see it.
4. **Practice Mindful Placement**: For a week, each time you return home or finish using a frequently-lost item, pause for three seconds as you place it in its designated spot. Notice the action, the color or texture of the bowl or hook, and the relief in knowing where your item is.

Over time, using these landing pads becomes a habit. You'll still have the occasional slip-up (hey, ADHD is persistent), but even partial success can drastically reduce those "Who moved my keys?" panic moments.

Strategy 2: The Art of Mindful Decluttering

Organizing clutter is like rearranging deck chairs on the Titanic if you have too much stuff to begin with. Mindful decluttering ensures you're fully present when deciding what stays and what goes, preventing the keep–toss cycle from spiraling into guilt or overwhelm.

How to Declutter Mindfully

1. **Set the Mood**: Declutter in a calm environment. Put on soothing music, light a candle—whatever helps you feel grounded. This isn't about punishing yourself for having "too much junk," but rather about choosing what truly serves you.
2. **Handle One Item at a Time**: Pick up an item, feel its weight, consider its purpose. Ask, *"Does this spark joy or serve a clear function?"* If not, set it aside for donation or recycling.
3. **Resist Autopilot**: Avoid moving items from one cluttered spot to another "for now." Instead, make a deliberate decision: keep, toss, donate, or store properly.
4. **Celebrate Small Wins**: Finished decluttering one drawer or shelf? Pause for a moment to appreciate the newly cleared space before moving on. That positive feeling can fuel your motivation.

Remember, mindful decluttering is a process. You might only tackle one dresser drawer or one kitchen cabinet at a time. The key is to be fully present, making intentional choices rather than half-heartedly shuffling items around.

Strategy 3: Squirrel Brain Meets Single-Tasking

You know that feeling: you start organizing your closet, then find a box of holiday decorations, which reminds you that you need new wrapping paper, which leads you online to shop, which leads to reading reviews for a vacuum cleaner you might need next year. ADHD squirrels your attention, scattering your focus across multiple tasks. Mindful organization champions **single-tasking**—focusing on one thing at a time.

How to Practice Single-Task Organization

1. **Pick One Zone**: Decide on a small, specific target—like the nightstand drawer or the coffee table surface.
2. **Set a Timer**: Give yourself 15–20 minutes (or whatever interval works) to work *only* on that zone.
3. **Minimize Distractions**: Turn off notifications. If you're at risk of meandering, set your phone out of arm's reach.
4. **Stay Curious and Engaged**: Each item you handle, ask yourself, "Do I need this here, or does it belong elsewhere? Does it still serve me?" This internal conversation keeps your mind from drifting.

If you notice you've wandered off into a different room or a different task, gently bring yourself back to the chosen zone—much like returning to your breath during meditation. This is the essence of mindfulness: noticing when you drift and guiding yourself back without judgment.

Strategy 4: Use Mini Mindfulness Breaks to Reset

ADHD minds can "max out" on focus. Maybe you've been sorting papers for a solid 15 minutes, and now your brain starts craving novelty. Instead of pushing until you're frazzled, schedule **mini mindfulness breaks** to recharge.

Sample Mini Break Routine

1. **Pause the Task**: Stand or sit quietly.
2. **Take Three Deep Breaths**: Inhale for four counts, hold for four, exhale for four, hold for four.
3. **Check In with Your Body**: Notice any tension in your shoulders, neck, or jaw. Release it if you can.
4. **Set an Intention**: "I will return to organizing for five more minutes."

By punctuating your work with these mini-breaks, you mitigate the mental fatigue that often causes ADHDers to abandon tasks halfway. This technique also helps you practice self-awareness, noticing your body and mental state rather than bulldozing through until burnout.

Strategy 5: Anchor Mindfulness in Daily Routines

For mindfulness to truly help your organization, it has to show up consistently—especially in routines you tend to skip or rush. Consider linking mindfulness to existing daily tasks:

1. **Morning "Keys Check"**: Each morning before you leave the house, consciously pause to locate keys, wallet, phone. Say out loud, "Keys? Check. Wallet? Check. Phone? Check." This quick verbal confirmation can ground you in the moment.
2. **End-of-Day 5-Minute Tidy**: Set a timer for five minutes each evening to straighten up your main living area. As you do, notice each object, placing it where it belongs. Mindfully pay attention to what you're touching and why.
3. **Meal Prep Mindfulness**: When unloading groceries or prepping meals, take a brief second to label the items out loud or in your head: "Tomatoes go here, yogurt goes here." The verbal repetition cements the action and location in your memory.

By weaving mindfulness into tasks you already perform—like leaving the house or tidying at night—you'll create an organized baseline that's easier to maintain.

Strategy 6: Gentle Self-Talk During the Process

Remember from previous chapters that harsh self-criticism can derail progress. A mindful approach to organization involves **gentle self-talk**. Instead of berating yourself for misplacing items, speak kindly:

- **"I'm learning a new way to place my things."**
- **"It's okay that I slipped this time; I'll remember next time."**
- **"I'm making small but meaningful progress."**

This supportive, compassionate tone can keep you engaged with the process rather than spiraling into shame or frustration when ADHD inevitably rears its head.

Real-Life Scenario: Casey's Mindful Keys

Casey, a marketing executive with ADHD, always lost her keys. Her mornings started with frantic searches, leaving her stressed before she even left the house. Fed up, she created a **"Keys Station"** on a small table by the door. She added a bright teal dish, hung a cheerful print above it, and placed a mini succulent for a calming vibe.

Each time Casey came home, she practiced the following steps:

1. **Pause**: She'd stand at the doorway for a second and notice her keys in her hand.
2. **Place**: She'd place the keys in the teal dish, saying, "Keys go here," under her breath.
3. **Breathe**: One deep inhale and exhale, acknowledging she was finishing the "arriving home" routine.

Over a few weeks, she found that she lost her keys significantly less. More importantly, the mindful ritual helped her decompress from the workday before plunging into any chaos at home. She transformed a once-stressful routine into a grounding, habit-forming micro-meditation.

Strategy 7: Environment Matters—Cues for Mindfulness

Mindful organization isn't just about controlling your mental state; your **physical environment** can support or sabotage your efforts. Use these environmental cues to stay present:

- **Strategic Signage**: Hang a small sign near your door that says, "Keys on the Hook?" or by your desk that says, "Check Your Calendar?" These gentle reminders can prompt quick moments of awareness.
- **Color Coding**: If you're prone to scattering items, color coding can make it easier to visually group them. For instance, all important documents go in a bright red folder, office supplies in a teal bin, etc.
- **Essential Oils or Scents**: Scents can anchor memories. If there's a particular scent (lavender, citrus) you find calming, use it near your main organization area. Each time you smell it, it can trigger a mindful pause.

When your environment is designed to remind you (rather than scold you), your ADHD brain has more consistent support for staying on task and remembering where things go.

Balancing Minimalism and Comfort

A mindful approach doesn't mean you have to become a ruthless minimalist or keep your home devoid of personal touches. **Comfort** matters—especially for an ADHD brain that thrives on pleasant or interesting stimuli. Strive for an environment that's **organized enough** to reduce stress, yet **inviting enough** that you actually enjoy being there.

- **Curate Decor**: Keep decorative items that genuinely spark joy or meaning. If that funky vase makes you smile, give it a proper, intentional place.
- **Rotate Extras**: Rather than displaying all your memorabilia or knick-knacks at once, consider rotating them. That way, you reduce visual clutter without sacrificing sentimental items.
- **Mindful Maintenance**: Every few months, do a quick inventory. Ask, "Is this still serving me or bringing joy?" If not, let it go mindfully.

Overcoming the "I Don't Have Time to Be Mindful" Myth

It's easy to think mindfulness requires sitting in silence for 30 minutes or mastering elaborate meditation techniques. In reality, mindfulness can be woven into your day in **tiny increments**—five seconds here, a minute there. The payoff? You save time on the back end by not frantically searching for lost items or reorganizing cluttered spaces repeatedly.

Micro-Mindfulness Moments

- **Hand on the Doorknob**: Before turning the knob, take one breath and notice your intention—leaving or entering.
- **Phone Check**: Each time you unlock your phone, pause for one second. Ask, "What am I here to do?" This can prevent a rabbit hole of distraction.
- **Laundry Folding**: Feel the texture of the clothes, notice the colors, and express gratitude you have clothes to fold—even if it's an annoying chore.

Think of mindfulness like a gentle companion, quietly guiding you to pay attention to your actions, your space, and your mood.

The Bigger Picture: Reduced Chaos, Increased Clarity

When mindful organization becomes part of your routine, something magical happens: **You reduce mental and emotional chaos**. Your ADHD brain no longer has to hold onto a dozen "Where did I put that?" mysteries. You free up bandwidth for creative projects, meaningful relationships, and restful downtime. Over time, the small mindful moments add up, creating a sense of calm and control you might've believed was out of reach.

Give Yourself Grace

Remember that ADHD is a lifelong condition—there is no "cure," but there are strategies to manage its impact. Some days, you'll forget to place your keys on the hook. Some weeks, you'll backslide into scattered piles around the house. **That's okay.** The goal isn't perfection but rather a gentle consistency that supports your daily life. Each time you come back to mindfulness, you're practicing a form of self-compassion and reinforcing the belief that you can—and will—get back on track.

Closing Thoughts

Mindful organization isn't about turning your home into a minimalist art gallery or becoming a Zen master. It's about sprinkling awareness into everyday routines so you know where your keys are (most of the time) and can tackle clutter without sending your stress hormones through the roof. When you embrace the power of slow, purposeful actions, you transform the mundane tasks of life into moments of self-care and mental clarity.

Sure, you might still have a squirrel or two scampering around your brain—this *is* ADHD, after all. But now you can gently guide those squirrels into a calmer, more structured habitat. And perhaps, one day, you'll pause while dropping your keys in their special dish, smile to yourself, and realize that you've learned to navigate your uniquely wired mind with grace and good humor.

9

Finding Your Flow in Work & Personal Projects

You sit down to write a report or tackle that long-postponed craft project. Within minutes, you're either completely in the zone—time fades away, and productivity skyrockets—or you're distracted by the slightest ping from your phone. For many women with ADHD, it can feel like there's no in-between: either you're riding the wave of hyperfocus or floundering in a sea of interrupted thoughts. *Flow* refers to that delicious state of full absorption in a task, where creativity blossoms, hours fly by, and you emerge feeling energized rather than drained. Yet how do you reliably reach that state with an ADHD brain that's prone to wandering?

In this chapter, we'll discuss what flow is, why it can be both a superpower and a challenge for ADHDers, and how to design your environment and routines to invite a more consistent flow—whether it's for your 9-to-5 job, a side hustle, or a passion project. We'll cover everything from leveraging your natural rhythms to creating ADHD-friendly task structures that ensure you spend less time battling distractions and more time immersed in the work that truly lights you up.

Understanding Flow—and Why It Matters for ADHD

Hungarian psychologist Mihaly Csikszentmihalyi coined the term "flow" to describe moments of **optimal experience**—when you're so focused on an activity that you lose self-consciousness and become one with the task. You might recall times when you were writing, painting, coding, organizing, or even cleaning, and suddenly two hours vanished in the blink of an eye. That's flow at its finest.

The ADHD Connection

For ADHD brains, hyperfocus can look remarkably similar to flow: you become captivated by a project, to the exclusion of all else. This trait can be an incredible asset—leading to leaps of creativity, rapid skill acquisition, or near-obsessive deep dives into a subject. But it can also cause problems if it's directed at the *wrong* things (e.g., binge-watching reality TV the night before a major deadline).

Key Differences Between Flow and ADHD Hyperfocus

- **Flow** typically includes a sense of progress and mastery; you're meeting a challenge that's just at the edge of your abilities.
- **ADHD Hyperfocus** can occur simply because something is novel or stimulating—even if it's not aligned with your goals or skill development.

Still, these two states share enough overlap that tapping into one often helps you experience the other. In other words, if you can intentionally steer your ADHD-fueled focus toward tasks that genuinely matter, you can harness the best of both worlds.

Strategy 1: Identify Your Peak Energy Cycles

Your brain and body operate on cycles that shift throughout the day—commonly referred to as **circadian rhythms**. For some, mornings are prime time for focus, while others hit their stride in the afternoon or late at night. Knowing your personal peak energy times is crucial for scheduling tasks that require deep engagement or creativity.

How to Discover Your Rhythm

1. **Track Energy and Focus**: For one to two weeks, jot down how alert or tired you feel at various points in the day. Use a simple 1–10 scale every couple of hours.
2. **Note Patterns**: Do you see a spike in motivation around 10 a.m. or a slump right after lunch? Are you inexplicably productive at 9 p.m.?
3. **Assign Tasks Accordingly**: Whenever possible, schedule your most challenging or creative tasks during your natural peak hours, and do simpler or more administrative tasks during your lower-energy times.

Overcoming Reality Constraints

Of course, real life doesn't always cater to your ideal schedule—especially if you work a 9-to-5 job or juggle family obligations. Still, any small adjustments help. For example, if your boss expects a certain project by Friday, you can aim to do the more complex portions during your higher-energy windows, even if that means arriving at the office a bit earlier or carving out a quiet hour after dinner.

Strategy 2: Design Tasks with Clear Goals and Immediate Feedback

Flow thrives when you know **exactly** what you're trying to accomplish and you can see (or sense) progress as you go. For ADHD minds prone to wandering, fuzzy or overly broad tasks can lead to frustration and lost momentum.

The Anatomy of a Flow-Friendly Task

1. **Specific Objective**: Instead of "Work on novel," try "Draft 500 words for the next chapter."
2. **Slight Challenge**: The task should be challenging enough to engage your brain but not so daunting that you freeze up.
3. **Immediate Feedback Loop**: This could be a word count, a checklist, or a visual meter that shows how far you've come. Your brain loves knowing "I'm 70% done."

Breaking It Down

If your project is inherently massive—like creating a business plan—break it into mini-milestones with tangible checkpoints. Celebrate each checkpoint with a quick mental pat on the back or a small reward. ADHD brains are more likely to remain engaged when they get frequent hits of progress-based satisfaction.

Strategy 3: Create a Flow-Conducive Environment

Just as you'd set the stage for a romantic dinner with dim lighting and soft music, you can "set the stage" for flow by optimizing your environment. ADHDers often do best with **structured** surroundings that reduce distractions while still offering some stimulation.

Lighting, Sound, and Clutter Control

- **Lighting**: Aim for natural light if possible. If that's not an option, use soft, warm-toned bulbs. Overly harsh lighting can irritate sensitive ADHD minds, while dim lighting might make you sleepy.
- **Sound**: Some people thrive with background noise (like instrumental music or a white-noise app). Others need near silence. Experiment to find your sweet spot.
- **Clutter**: While a minimalist workspace might work wonders for some, others find a bit of visual interest sparks creativity. Strike a balance—keep your immediate work area clear enough that you're not overwhelmed, but allow for items that inspire you (mood board, decorative trinkets, etc.).

Guarding Against Distractions

- **Notification Settings**: Turn off unnecessary pings or alerts on your devices. Constant digital interruptions are flow killers.
- **Physical Boundaries**: If possible, designate a specific area (even a tiny corner) that signals "focus mode." Communicate to family or roommates that when you're in this space,

you'd prefer not to be interrupted—unless it's urgent.

Strategy 4: Harness Hyperfocus Wisely

When hyperfocus strikes an ADHD brain, it's like rocket fuel—catapulting you into deep engagement. The trick is ensuring that rocket fuel is directed at tasks that align with your priorities, rather than random internet rabbit holes.

Scheduling Hyperfocus

- **Identify Tasks That Spark Interest**: Hyperfocus often kicks in for tasks you find genuinely interesting. So, if you can align your work or project with your personal curiosities, you increase the chance of slipping into flow.
- **Time-Block It**: If possible, block off a chunk of your schedule (an hour, two hours, etc.) specifically for that task. Let family members or coworkers know you'll be "offline" or unavailable during that window.
- **Set Multiple Alarms**: Hyperfocus can make you lose track of time, so set alarms at intervals to prompt you to check if you need a break, to hydrate, or to switch tasks if necessary.

Accept the Downsides

Even with careful planning, hyperfocus can sometimes cause you to forget meals or skip other important tasks. You may need to build "safeguards" into your environment—like scheduling reminders to stand up and stretch, or placing a water bottle within arm's reach. Hyperfocus isn't inherently good or bad; it's all about how you channel and manage it.

Strategy 5: Embrace Mindful Transitioning

One overlooked aspect of flow is **how you move in and out** of it. ADHD brains often struggle with task-switching or shifting gears—what was once a productive flow session can become a 5-hour rabbit hole if you never transition to your next priority.

The Power of Routines and Rituals

- **Pre-Flow Ritual**: Spend a minute or two setting an intention: "For the next 30 minutes, I will draft my presentation slides." This can involve a short breathing exercise or clearing your desk of unrelated items.
- **Post-Flow Check-In**: After your session, take a brief moment to note what you accomplished and how you feel. Jot down any tasks that emerged during your flow that you need to address later. This helps your ADHD brain *offload* the mental clutter.

Gentle Alarms and Cues

When you're in the zone, an abrupt alarm can feel jarring, pulling you out of flow too harshly. Consider using soothing chimes or music that gradually fades in. A subtle cue can help you wrap up gracefully rather than ripping you out of a productive trance.

Strategy 6: Leverage Collaborative Flow

Sometimes, working with others can amplify your concentration. **Body doubling**—where you sit with another person who's also focusing on a task—can significantly boost ADHD productivity. Collaboration or co-working sessions can foster a sense of communal flow, where everyone keeps each other anchored.

Virtual Co-Working and Accountability

If you don't have someone physically nearby to co-work with, try virtual alternatives. Many online communities schedule "focus sprints," where people join a video call, briefly state their goals, then work in silence or muted chatter for a set period before regrouping to share progress. This external accountability often helps ADHDers stay on task and maintain flow longer than they would solo.

Strategy 7: Navigating Flow in Personal vs. Professional Contexts

ADHD women juggle multiple roles—employee, entrepreneur, parent, partner, friend, hobbyist. Flow might come more naturally in certain areas (like painting or gaming) than in others (like expense reports or house chores). Recognize that different contexts may require slightly different approaches.

Flow at Work

- **Clarify Your Role**: Are your job duties vague? Advocate for clearer objectives. If your boss hands you broad projects, request specific milestones or deliverables.
- **Delegate or Collaborate**: Tasks that feel draining or tedious can be delegated if possible. Alternatively, find a coworker who enjoys that aspect and swap tasks. Minimizing drudgery frees up mental energy for deeper engagement.

Flow in Hobbies

- **Give Yourself Permission**: Many women feel guilty about spending time on personal interests when there's a never-ending to-do list. But flow is recharging, and pursuing hobbies can reduce ADHD stress.
- **Keep It Purposeful**: If you're crocheting, building furniture, or writing fan fiction, set micro-goals to track your progress—like completing one pattern or finishing a chapter. This helps you maintain momentum and see tangible growth.

Flow in Daily Life

Flow doesn't have to be about big projects—it can also enhance everyday tasks. Some people find a sweet spot while cooking, tidying, or gardening. If a daily chore occasionally sparks flow, lean into it! Turn on music, set a small challenge (e.g., "Can I reorganize this drawer in 15 minutes while dancing to my favorite playlist?"), and let yourself enjoy the process.

Real-Life Story: Maya's Flow-Focused Writing Routine

Maya, an account manager by day and aspiring novelist by night, struggled to write consistently. She'd often wait for the elusive "perfect moment" to feel inspired, which rarely came. Frustrated, she decided to apply the principles of flow:

1. **Rhythm Discovery**: Maya realized she felt most alert from 6 a.m. to 8 a.m.
2. **Environment Tweaks**: She cleared her kitchen table each night, so she could start fresh in the morning. She also set up a soft-light lamp and curated a "focus playlist" of instrumental piano tracks.
3. **Task Design**: She gave herself a mini-goal: write 500 words or one scene, whichever came first. This was specific, mildly challenging, and offered immediate feedback (the word count ticked up).
4. **Mindful Start**: Each morning, Maya brewed coffee, sat down, took three deep breaths, and repeated, "I'm here to write 500 words." She silenced her phone for 60 minutes.
5. **Gentle Wrap-Up**: Once she hit her 500 words or the hour expired, she saved her document, jotted notes for the next scene, and stretched. If she still felt the flow, she'd continue, but that short routine was non-negotiable.

Within weeks, Maya noticed she slipped into a flow state more consistently. She finished her novel draft in three months—a task that once felt impossible. The combination of mindful routines, environment, and clear goals helped her ADHD brain engage with her writing instead of drifting.

The Role of Self-Compassion in Finding Flow

Even with these strategies, there'll be days when your ADHD mind refuses to cooperate. Maybe you just can't get into the zone, or you hyperfocus on the wrong thing. This is normal—especially if your life is busy, you're under stress, or you didn't sleep well.

Embracing Imperfection

Flow isn't meant to be a 24/7 state. It's a fleeting experience that often emerges when conditions are right. If you chase flow too obsessively, you might fall into frustration or guilt on days it doesn't happen. Practice self-compassion:

- **Acknowledge the Context**: Stress, illness, or emotional upheaval can impede flow, no matter how perfectly you schedule your day.
- **Focus on the Process**: Even if you don't feel that magical immersion, showing up consistently to your routine counts as progress.
- **Celebrate Micro-Victories**: Finished half your planned work? That's still a victory. Wrote 200 words instead of 500? Better than none.

When you're kind to yourself, you reduce the mental friction that often blocks flow in the first place.

Reclaim Your Creativity and Productivity

Flow is more than a productivity hack; it's a path to deeper satisfaction and even joy in your work and personal projects. For women with ADHD, achieving flow can be transformative—replacing frustration and scattered half-finished ideas with purposeful engagement and tangible achievements.

Put It into Practice

1. **Pick One Strategy**: Maybe you'll experiment with identifying your peak energy hours, or design a flow-friendly environment. Start small.
2. **Track Shifts**: Notice any improvements in focus, satisfaction, or output.
3. **Refine, Repeat**: If a method doesn't work right away, tweak it. ADHD minds need a bit of trial and error to find the perfect recipe.

The goal here isn't to become a productivity machine—far from it. Rather, it's to tap into your innate capacity for passionate, focused work—whether that's building a career you love, finishing a knitting project, or writing the next great novel. By aligning your tasks, environment, and mindset, you give yourself permission to lean into that absorbing, fulfilling state of flow. And in doing so, you might just discover new reservoirs of creativity and resilience you never knew you had.

10

Celebrate the (Imperfect) Wins

You glance around your living room—there's a basket of laundry that didn't quite get folded, a stack of mail waiting to be sorted, and a half-finished craft project on the coffee table. In another moment, you might see this as *further evidence* of an ADHD brain that never seems to get fully organized. But today, you notice something different: that mountain of laundry is smaller than it used to be. The mail stack is half the size, and the craft project is (mostly) contained on its own tray. There's less clutter, fewer frantic searches for lost items, and a calmer undercurrent to your daily routine.

This, dear reader, is what we call an **imperfect win**—the kind that often goes unnoticed because we're conditioned to see only the tasks we haven't finished or the clutter that isn't fully tamed. Yet these small, incremental improvements are exactly what deserve celebrating. They tell the story of how far you've come, how many new strategies you've tried, and the ways you've learned to accommodate (and even embrace) your ADHD quirks.

In this final chapter, we'll delve into the art of celebrating these messy-yet-meaningful victories. We'll also explore how to keep momentum going, pivot when life inevitably changes, and chart a path forward that honors both your ADHD challenges and your undeniable strengths.

The Importance of Celebrating Small Wins

If there's one thing that can keep an ADHD mind from feeling perpetually behind, it's recognizing the progress you've already made. Research in psychology emphasizes that **positive reinforcement** and **recognition** of success can fuel motivation far more effectively than constant reminders of shortcomings.

Why ADHDers Need Celebration More Than Ever

- **Motivation Fuel**: Your ADHD brain thrives on dopamine, that feel-good chemical often released when you achieve a goal. Celebrations—no matter how small—can give a quick burst of that rewarding sensation.
- **Counteracting Negative Loops**: Many women with ADHD carry years of self-criticism. Celebrating wins, however imperfect, disrupts those negative feedback loops.
- **Building Resilience**: Acknowledging incremental progress creates a buffer against future setbacks. When you stumble, you'll recall that you've succeeded before and can do so again.

Think of each celebration as a deposit into your emotional bank account—money in the bank for when an inevitable rough patch comes along.

Strategy 1: Keep a "Wins" Journal

You might already track appointments or to-dos in a planner or digital calendar. Why not apply the same method to your **successes**? The act of writing them down cements the experience in your mind.

How to Start

1. **Choose Your Format**: A simple notebook, a digital note on your phone, or a fancy bullet journal page—pick whatever you'll stick with.
2. **Set a Prompt**: Each evening (or morning), jot down at least one win. It could be as small as "I put my keys on the hook every day this week" or as big as "I finally tackled the taxes I'd been avoiding for months."
3. **Include Feelings**: When you record a win, note how it felt—relief, pride, excitement. Linking the achievement to an emotional response makes the memory more powerful.

Over time, you'll have a personal record of progress. On days when you feel like you're back at square one, leaf through your wins journal to remind yourself that growth is never truly lost.

Strategy 2: Adopt a Progress-Over-Perfection Mindset

Throughout this book, we've underscored the importance of **progress over perfection**. Let's dig a little deeper into what that looks like in practice.

Defining "Good Enough"

1. **Set Realistic Standards**: If your goal was to reduce clutter, maybe "good enough" means you can find all essential items (keys, wallet, phone) without searching frantically each morning.
2. **Acknowledge Bandwidth**: Some weeks, you'll have the energy to organize every drawer in your home office; other weeks, a single shelf might be all you can manage. Both are valid forms of progress.
3. **Celebrate "Almost Done"**: If you sorted 70% of your paperwork, that's still 70% more than before. A partial victory is better than no victory at all.

Uncoupling Worth from Output

One trap for many ADHD women is tying self-esteem to productivity. *"If I don't accomplish X, I'm failing."* Instead, focus on your own incremental forward movement. Even if you only manage a fraction of your to-do list, you're learning strategies that will pay off long-term. You are worthy no matter how many boxes get checked.

Strategy 3: Reflect on the Journey

It's easy to lose sight of how far you've come if you never look back. Reflection cements growth and gives you valuable data on what worked (and what didn't).

Reflection Questions

- **Which strategies have helped you most?** Think about the tools in previous chapters—did mindful organization transform your morning routine? Did micro-habits reduce clutter?
- **Where did you stumble?** Recognize challenges not as failures but as signposts. Did you struggle with procrastination after a stressful week? Did you forget your landing pad system when life got busy? Use these insights to refine your approach.
- **Who supported you?** Perhaps a friend, partner, online group, or coach. Acknowledge their part in your success. Gratitude not only builds relationships but also boosts your mood.

Scheduled Check-Ins

Plan to do a deeper reflection monthly or quarterly. By carving out dedicated time, you ensure you're not only focusing on the day-to-day hustle but also assessing your overall growth.

Strategy 4: Pivot When Life Changes

What happens when you move to a new home, switch jobs, have a child, or face an unexpected health crisis? ADHD management can get thrown for a loop. In these transitional times, it's crucial to revisit your systems—and celebrate any successes in navigating the upheaval.

Reassessing Your Systems

- **Environmental Changes**: New house means new landing pads. A job change might demand a fresh time-blocking strategy. Accept that a system that once worked might need tweaking or replacement.
- **Emotional Overload**: Major life changes can heighten ADHD symptoms. Double down on self-compassion and try smaller, more manageable tactics rather than overhauling everything at once.
- **Experiment with Alternatives**: If a color-coded planner used to be your mainstay but no longer fits your schedule, test digital apps, whiteboards, or hybrid systems. Keep an open mind until you find a comfortable fit again.

Marking Milestones

Celebrate not just the end result but the adaptability itself. Did you reorganize your new kitchen to be more ADHD-friendly? Cheer for that. Did you navigate two weeks of upheaval at work without forgetting critical deadlines? That's a major win. Life changes often reveal how resilient you are—and that's cause for celebration in itself.

Strategy 5: Incorporate Self-Care as Part of Your Wins

Self-care isn't a separate side quest; it's integral to sustaining the energy and mental clarity needed for ADHD management. If you burn out, even the best organization systems will crumble.

Linking Self-Care to Celebrations

- **Reward Yourself with Rest**: Instead of pushing through exhaustion, treat that midday nap or a leisurely bath as a well-earned reward for your recent organizational strides.
- **Mental Health Check-Ins**: Therapy sessions, journaling, or meditation can be forms of celebration. They affirm your commitment to personal growth, which is worth acknowledging as a win.
- **Physical Movement**: A fun dance class or a relaxing walk can double as both self-care and a celebration of the progress you've made—"I'm moving my body because I'm proud of what I've accomplished."

Celebratory Rituals

Maybe you create a small ritual after achieving a milestone—like enjoying your favorite dessert, visiting a local park, or reading an extra chapter of a book you love. These rituals signal to your brain: *"I did something good, and I deserve joy for it."*

Real-Life Story: Brianna's Laundry Victory

Brianna, a mother of two with ADHD, used to be overwhelmed by an ever-growing pile of laundry. After reading about microhabits, she decided to create a **Daily Laundry** rule: wash and dry one small load each night, fold it immediately after dinner, and put it away before bed.

For the first week, she succeeded three out of seven days. Initially, she felt like a failure—until she shifted her perspective toward "imperfect wins." *Three loads folded is a heck of a lot better than zero!* Over the following month, she averaged four or five successful laundry days each week. The pile shrank dramatically, and the mornings became calmer.

To celebrate, she took herself out for a solo coffee date each Sunday—no kids, no chores. This small ritual reinforced her progress. Even if she skipped laundry some nights, she recognized the overall improvement. That celebratory coffee became a symbol of her shifting mindset: from endless guilt to measured progress.

Strategy 6: Share Your Wins with a Support Network

You don't have to cheer for yourself alone. In fact, sharing your triumphs—big or small—with friends, family, or an ADHD-focused community can amplify the positive impact.

Why External Validation Helps

- **Accountability**: Knowing someone's waiting to hear your success story can motivate you to follow through on your micro-habits or decluttering goals.
- **Encouragement**: Loved ones might spot progress you're too modest (or critical) to see in yourself. Hearing them say "Wow, your living room looks so much more spacious!" can be a powerful reminder that you're making real changes.
- **Normalizing Imperfection**: In supportive ADHD circles or online forums, you'll find others celebrating small wins—like remembering to pay a bill on time or finishing a short reading assignment. That collective acceptance of imperfection reduces shame.

Choose Your Audience Carefully

While sharing can be uplifting, ensure you're doing so with people who genuinely understand or empathize with ADHD challenges. Unsupportive or overly critical voices can dampen your sense of achievement. Seek out a friend, coach, therapist, or community group where positivity and understanding are the norms.

Strategy 7: Sustain Your Momentum Beyond This Book

You've learned a host of strategies—from mindful organization to tiny habits, from tackling decision paralysis to embracing flow states. How do you keep these insights alive once you've turned the last page?

Ongoing Learning

- **Books & Resources**: Keep exploring other ADHD-focused literature, podcasts, or online courses. Each new perspective might offer a fresh tactic or reaffirm what you've learned.
- **Revisit Chapters**: Your ADHD journey will evolve. Re-reading sections—especially during life transitions—can spark new ideas or remind you of forgotten tactics.
- **Stay Curious**: ADHD brains crave novelty, so occasionally switch up your organizational systems or reward structures. This prevents boredom and keeps your engagement high.

Embrace Adaptive Flexibility

Rather than expecting any single system to serve you forever, treat your strategies as living, breathing entities. You'll adapt them as your schedule, environment, and personal growth change. Each time you do, celebrate the flexibility that keeps you moving forward instead of lamenting the fact that you had to change course again.

A Final Word on Imperfection

If there's one mantra to take with you, let it be: **"Imperfect doesn't mean 'not good enough.'"** A day with one small step forward is still progress. A home that's 70% organized instead of 100% is a massive improvement if you used to live in complete chaos. A to-do list with two items checked off instead of ten is still cause for a pat on the back.

ADHD management is a *continuous dance*—sometimes you lead, sometimes you follow, and sometimes you trip over your own feet. That's all part of the process. By celebrating the stumbling, the rebalancing, and every partial victory, you create a life where you're more aligned with your values, less burdened by shame, and freer to explore the world in all your vibrant, creative, ADHD glory.

Chapter Summary: A Toast to Your Wins

1. **Recognize Small Victories**: From placing your keys on a hook to decluttering a single drawer, each step forward is worth noting.
2. **Practice Progress Over Perfection**: Aim for "good enough"

rather than an unattainable standard of flawless organization.
3. **Reflect, Pivot, and Adapt**: Change is inevitable, so allow your systems and habits to evolve. Look back to see how far you've come.
4. **Share the Joy**: Let friends or supportive communities cheer you on. Collective encouragement multiplies the power of each success.
5. **Invest in Self-Care**: Whether it's a simple nap or a fun dance class, treat self-care as a celebration of the improvements you've made.
6. **Keep Learning**: The end of this book is not the end of your journey. Stay curious, experiment, and refine.

A Final Thank-You to Yourself

Before you close this book, pause and give yourself credit for making it this far. You invested time and energy in understanding your ADHD mind and shaping an environment and habits that support you. That alone is a massive accomplishment. So often, women with ADHD feel invisible or unheard, but here you are—showing up for yourself, determined to find strategies that resonate with your unique brain wiring.

Whether you've implemented every technique or just skimmed chapters for ideas, you've planted seeds of change. Keep watering them with self-compassion, consistent reflection, and a willingness to adapt. Over time, those seeds will grow into an organizational framework that's not perfect (and never needs to be) but is perfectly attuned to you.

www.ingramcontent.com/pod-product-compliance
Lightning Source LLC
Chambersburg PA
CBHW071720020426
42333CB00017B/2343